THE END

THE END

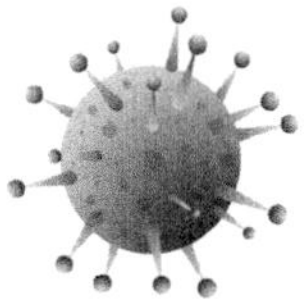

First Published April 2020

ISBN 978-1-9995850-7-5

Designed, Printed & Published by

www.designmarque.co.uk

ONLY
SARAH RAY
COULD HAVE TAKEN ON
THE CHALLENGING WORK
AND METICULOUS PRESENTATION
OF ALL OUR BOOKS
YOU ARE AMAZING

Thank you with love
Kev and Moe

Front cover image credit Moe Bura

DEDICATION

Love and respect for all our families

Someone died today of covid -19 virus and they will all be remembered as someone's son, daughter, aunt, uncle, cousin, husband, wife, friend, enemy, lover, teacher, leader, nurse, doctor, scientist, hairdresser, dentist, carer, author, publisher, driver, postman, sportsperson, actor, presenter, reporter, mother, father, grandparents, artist, musician, poet and every other human who contributed to life on Earth

We have been self isolating for 3 months and every day the news just reports a number relating to the dead which rises every day. We are trying to survive a global pandemic that no one can compare to anything that has ever happened before.

As vegans we are growing plant based food because the food we stored will not last long. Our family too are trying to stay safe with the knowledge we all share.

With the collapse of industry and the uncertainty about everything that we knew. It will fall on the shoulders of the survivors who will have to take on the challenges of building and repairing a better, kinder world for us all with
Peace Food Water Dreams

THE MAD HACKERS
Kev & Moe Bura

KEV BURA

KNEW WHAT HE MEANT
SAID WHAT HE THOUGHT
WROTE IT ALL DOWN
MADE SURE HE HAD TIME
TO MAKE IT ALL RHYME

With love and appreciation for my lifelong partner
who has shared an extraordinary amount
of time with me
Moe Bura

1

ONE IS A WALKER
A BIT OF A TALKER
BUT ONES NEVER BEEN
A PSYCHO STALKER
OUT ON THE STREET
WITH PEOPLE YOU MEET
SOME YOU'D LOVE TO EAT WITH
OTHERS ONE JUST GREETS
PASS ON PASS UP
PASS OUT OF SIGHT
ONES IN ONES ZONE
ONES IN ONES PRIME
ITS NOT ONES AGE
IT IS ONES TIME
TO TAKE HOLD OF ONES LIFE
AND HOLD ON FOR THE RIDE
ONES IN CONTROL
FOR THE FIRST TIME IN ONES LIFE
ONES SHACKLES ARE OFF
ALONG WITH ONES BAGGAGE AND STRIFE
TODAY IS ONES FIRST DAY
ONE IS PRESENTLY SURPRISED
ONES CHOSEN ONES FUTURE
WITH ONES LOVE STRENGTH AND PRIDE
PSYCHO STALKERS
INTERNET TALKERS
SOLICITING PERSONAL DATA FORUMS
MAKING CONVERSATIONS
IT'S JUST COMMUNICATIONS
PERPETRATORS OF BODY AND MIND
RADICALISATION
PRE AND POST HYPNOTIC SUGGESTIONS
CONTROL THE MIND
CONTROL THE PERSON

CONTROL THE CROWD
CONTROL THE STUDIO AUDIENCE
CONTROL THE MEDIA
AND THE BROADCASTERS PATIENCE
INCITEMENT TO HATE
INCITEMENT TO LIE
INCITEMENT TO CAUSE
ANTI-SEMITISM CALLS
INCITEMENT OF RELIGIONS
TO SPLIT AND DIVIDE
WHILE SOME MAY PREFER
THE PIG BARREL POLITICAL RIDE

2

FRANCE'S VESTED INTEREST
IS IN IT'S OWN PEOPLES

3

ELEPHANTS NEVER FORGET
LIKE GRANDCHILDREN RECEIVING
BIRTHDAY PRESENTS FROM GRANDPARENTS
WHO ARE JUST LIKE OLD ELEPHANTS

4

ONE IS A MUG
IF ONE BELIEVES
EVERYONE OUT THERE
IS THEIR CUP OF TEA

5

MADURO GUAIDO
GUAIDO MADURO
VENEZUELA GOES LIKE BRAZIL
U S A BACK GUAIDO
VENEZUELA VOTED MADURO

6

WHY IS A PRINCE
ALWAYS A PRINCE
WHEN A PRINCE IS
THE PRINCIPAL CULPRIT
IN A ROAD TRAFFIC ACCIDENT
INVOLVING TWO WOMEN
ONE A MOTHER
WITH 9 MONTH OLD CHILD
THE QUEEN BUYS PRINCE PHILLIP
THE NEXT DAY A NEW CAR
THE MOTHER AND CHILD RECEIVE
A GET WELL CARD

7

ONE MUST ASSUME BILLIONAIRES
PAY THEIR TAXES EVEN
THOUGH THEIR MONEY FLOWS
THROUGH OFF SHORE TAX HAVENS

8

THERE IS ENOUGH HYPOCRISY
TO GO AROUND THE WORLD
OF ALL COUNTRIES ESPECIALLY
THOSE THAT MANUFACTURE
AND SELL ARMS AND AMMUNITIONS
LIKE THE BRITISH GOVERNMENT
OF CONSERVATIVES WHO HAVE SOLD
THIS YEAR OVER FIVE BILLION POUNDS
WORTH OF AMMUNITIONS TO
ONE OF THE RICHEST COUNTRIES
SAUDI ARABIA WHO IN TURN HAVE
DROPPED THAT OBSCENE AMOUNT
OF AMMUNITIONS ON THEIR NEIGHBOUR
YEMAN WHO ARE ONE OF THE WORLDS
POOREST COUNTRIES AND SO AS
THIS GOVERNMENT LICKS THE ARSE
OF SAUDI PRINCES
OUR BRITISH FORCES AND CHARITIES LICKS
THE WOUNDS OF THE YEMAN PEOPLES

9

LIAM NEESON'S INDOCTRINATION IN NORTHERN IRELAND
MADE LIAM SEE HE WAS WRONG
AFTER A WEEK A RACIST HE IS NOT
HE HAS CHANGED HIS SONG
AS LOVE OF ALL RACES
IS THE WAY TO LIVE ON

10

WATER WAVES
HEAT WAVES
PLANTS WAVE
WINDS WAVE
BLOWING WAVES OF EMOTIONS
BLOWING WAVES OF FEAR
BLOWING WAVES OF PASSION
MAKING WAVES TO APPEAR
OF PEOPLES MARCHING
PEOPLE COLLECTIVELY CHEER
FOR THE END OF AUSTERITY
FOR THE END OF CHEAP JOBS
EXPENSIVE HOUSES AND DEBT
LET US ALL BE CLEAR
OUR ELEPHANTS ARE IN PRISMS
HOLD ON EVERYONE
ON THE WAVE OF SOCIALISM

11

HOMELESS AND DOWN
LIKE CANS IN A GUTTER
LIKE PLASTIC ON SHORELINES
LIKE PLASTIC PARTICLES IN SEAS
DAWN OF A BEGINNING
WHERE LIFE HAD SOME MEANING
WHERE ONE COULD RELY ON
LIVING ONES LIFE FREE
BEGINNING ONES END
IS TO HAVE LIVED FROM ONES BEGINNING
TO HAVE LOVED ONES MEANING OF LIFE
AND BE ABLE TO COMPREHEND

12

LIKE RAIN AND RIVERS
BLOOD FLOWS LIKE STREAMS
LIFE FORCE LIFES DREAMS
LIVING CREATURES FISH IT SEEMS
LIFE MAY HAVE EMERGED
FROM THE STREAM
AND CRAWLED OUT AND BECAME
OTHER SPECIES ANIMALS MAYBE
AND HERE ON EARTHS
MERRY GO ROUND OF ORBITS
MANS DREAMS ARE FAR OFF
INTO OUTER SPACE
SEARCHING FOR LIFE MORE LIFE
OUR LIFE BEAUTIFUL ENOUGH TO SAVE
TO ME

13

THE HUNK OF A PUNK ON SKUNK WITH JUNK
SAID TO THE DRUNK MONK ON THE BUNK
DO YOU DIG FUNK

14

HERE WE ALL ARE
WE'VE BEEN DIVIDED AND RULED
SUPPRESSED FOOLED AND RIDICULED
BY A TAX LESS OVER PAID FEW
WHO ARE NOT LIKE ME OR YOU

15

LIVING HAND TO MOUTH
ONE SEES FRUSTRATION ALL ABOUT
ONE COULD BE LIVING NORTH OR SOUTH
EXTREMITY POVERTY SHOUTS
LOW WAGE LOW PAID LIVING AGE
NO WAY OF LIVING ON A LOW WAGE
THERES NOTHING TO SAY
THERES NOTHING TO EAT
THE FOOD BANKS WHERE
FOOD COMES FROM TO MOST KIDS
TO MANY TOO MANY CASUAL JOBS
ADDS TO THE FRUSTRATIONS
ONE DOESN'T HAVE TWO BOBS
TO RUB TOGETHER
CAN'T PAY ONES WAY
ALL DAYS ARE RAINY DAYS
POURING ONES HEART OUT
WRINGING IT OUT ONE SAYS
ONES GOING TO HELP ONES NEIGHBOURS
COLLECTIVELY BE AND SEE THE SOCIALISTS WAY

16

MICHAEL PARKINSON
WAS ONE OF BRITAINS
FIRST AND FINEST T V INTERVIEWERS
OF THE 20th CENTURY
TO SIR BILLY AND ME
TAKING THE MICKY IS APPROPRIATELY
APPLIED TO ALL SUFFERERS OF
PARKINSON'S DISEASE

17

WE ARE PREPARED TO GO TO WAR
TO POSSESS AND PROCURE THE HEROINE POPPY
BUT THE MARIJUANA PLANT IS TRASHED AND BURNED
BY THE SAME HYPOCRITICAL ARMY

18

PRIME MINISTER
TONY CHARLES MIRANDA LINTON BLAIR
LIED TO A FULL HOUSE OF COMMONS
AND LED BRITAIN INTO WARFARE
IF THAT WAS NOT BAD ENOUGH
THIS MAYBE WORST THE CULPABLE COVER UP
FOR 100 YEARS NO ONE CAN READ THE FILES
OF THE 2002 POLICE INVESTIGATION INTO
WESTMINSTERS P A E D O P H I L E S

19

DENIS CORPET IN 2014
DISCOVERED THE LINK BETWEEN
CANCER AND PROCESSED MEATS
RED MEATS FULL OF NITRITES
LIKE BACON HAM DELI MEATS AND CORNED BEEF
THE LACK OF INTUITIVE ADVISING
PROGRAMS OF EDUCATION
INFORMING THE PUBLIC OF THEIR
HEALTH AND WELFARE
IS TESTIMONY OF CONSERVATIVE GOVERNMENTS
DERELICTION OF DUTY

20

THE PATRONISING INTIMIDATING BIGOTRY
SPOKEN BY POMPOUS RELIGIOUS ARSE SOULS
SHOULD BY LAW BE MADE TO SPEAK
ONLY TO ONE ANOTHER

21

ALTHOUGH THE END CRASH OF MAYS
CAPITALIST GOVERNMENT DRAWS NEAR
NO ONE CAN PREDICT
WHEN OR WHERE BUT ALL FEAR
THE WORST CASE SCENARIO
BANKRUPT IN DEBT UP TO HERE
LEAVING BORIS AND COMPANY
TO CLEAN UP EVEN MORE MY DEARS

22

HYPOCRISY
IF ONE IS PRIVILEGED AND RICH
ONE IS MORE THAN ABLE
TO PAY ONES FINE
MORE THAN ENOUGH
NOT TO DO TIME
IF ONE IS A PRINCE
AND OVER TURNS ONES CAR
HITTING ANOTHER
THE LAW WILL NOT TAKE IT TOO FAR
KEEPING WITH PRINCES
IN PRINCIPALITIES OVER SEAS

THEY TAKE DRUGS AND DRINK ALCOHOL
IN THEIR BASEMENTS ONE IS TO BELIEVE
IF ONE IS THE WRONG COLOUR
POOR YOUNG OR OLD
OF THE WRONG ORIENTATION OF SEXUAL
ONE CAN BE CHARGED NICKED AND
DEFINED A CRIMINAL

23

ONE SHOULD KNOW
WHAT ONE PUTS IN ONES BODY
THE END RESULT
IS A LOAD OF CRAP
THAT'S AFTER OF COURSE
ALL THE BEST BITS THE NUTRIENTS
ARE ALL TAKEN OUT
ITS LIKE ALL NEWS AND INFORMATION
DECIPHERED TRANSLATED
AND INTERPRETED AS IT SPOUTS
THE FACTS FROM FICTION
THE FILMS ON TELEVISION
THE TRUTH OR PROPAGANDA
THE POMPOUS GOSSIP
OF BILLIONAIRE GANGSTERS
LET THEIR FOLLY
LEAD TO ONES PREDICTION
WHO WRITES FICTION
WHO WRITES FACTS
WHO WRITES TRUTH
WHO WRITES CRAP
DON'T BUY NEWSPAPERS
THEY'RE FULL OF ALL OF THAT
THE TRUTH IS
THE FICTION OF THE FACTS
AND THATS THEIR CRAP

24

AS A TSUNAMI WAVE OF CRITICISM
ROLLS IN OFF THE SEA
THAT BORIS'S GOVERNMENT HAS ALREADY BEEN
WRITTEN DOWN IN HISTORY
POST APOCALYPTIC DENIAL OF CLIMATE
CHANGE THE FACTS
SOCIALLY GROW AS ONE GROWS
TREES AND FOOD WITH CLEAN STREAMS
BUILD HOUSES FIX THE INFRASTRUCTURE
CREATE CREATE ONES DREAMS
EARTH IS GOING NOWHERE
ONES FUTURE IS NEAR
FOR WE ARE ALL DINOSAURS
WE SHALL ALL LEAVE OUR SHIT
FOR THE NEXT GENERATION
THAT MAY POSSIBLY FOLLOW
TO CLEAN UP ENOUGH WASTE
FOR THEMSELVES TO SHIT

25

THERE IS NO EXCUSE
IT MAKES ONE PEUKE
TO SEE SO MANY KIDS
WITH FAT KNEES THEY'RE OBESE
EDUCATION IS OUT THERE
SEE TOO MANY STILL DRINKING BUBBLES
YEAH FULL OF SUGARS
SWEETENERS WORST STILL
IT KEEPS ONE COMING BACK
LIKE ON PILLS WORST STILL CRACK

KICK THE SUGARS AND SALTS
GET THEM OUT FOR A WALK
NO ONE NEEDS
ANIMAL PRODUCTS IN ONES DIET
CHANGE OF MIND TIME TO CHANGE
ENOUGH BODY BAGGAGE
ONE AND ALL MUST REFRAIN
FROM EATING FAST MEAT BURGERS
FROM EATING FAST CHICKEN WINGERS
FROM DRINKING FAST MILK SHAKERS
THEY'RE JUST CALF HORMONE GROWTH SHAKES
THEY ALL CAUSE ONE TO BE OBESE
THEY ALL CAUSE ONE TO HAVE FAT KNEES
THEY ALL CAUSE MAN TO CHOP DOWN TREES
THEY ALL CAUSE CLIMATE CHANGE
THE FARMERS THE CORPORATIONS
AND THE GOVERNMENTS THROUGH THEIR
DERELICTION OF DUTY
TO INFORM REFORM AND CHANGE

26

WORDS MAYBE MANY
WORDS MAYBE FEW
WORDS MAYBE RED
WORDS MAYBE BLUE
WORDS MAYBE HONEST FAIR OR TRUE
WORDS MAYBE LIES BAD AND UNTRUTHS
WORDS MAYBE EVIL CORRUPT TO CONFUSE
WORDS THAT MAYBE SPOKEN
BY ONE AND ALL LIKE ONESELF IS THIS NOT TRUE

27

CHINESE SCIENTISTS CELEBRATE
CHINESE SUCCESS IN SPACE
IT'S A FAR CRY FROM EARTH
THE FAR SIDE OF THE MOON
WHERE A 9 MILE CRATER IS TO BE EXPLORED
AND ERECT A TELESCOPE TO ZOOM
OUT FURTHER INTO OUR GALAXY
AND BEYOND OUR FUTURE
LIFE ON EARTH CLINGS ON
AS CLIMATE CHANGES AND
VIRAL WARS ARE SET UPON

28

SCREEN ONES EYES
FROM THE SCREEN
EYES ARE BETTER OUTSIDE
SO IT SEEMS
CHILDREN'S EYES ESPECIALLY
THEY'RE STILL GROWING AND NEED
PROTECTION AND GUIDANCE
FOR THEIR POTENTIAL TO SEE

29

DRIVING ON THE QUEENS HIGHWAY
ONE WONDERS WHETHER THE QUEEN PAYS HER TAX
ALONG WITH HER INSURANCE IF SO
ONE WOULD LOVE TO KNOW HOW MUCH

30

PARANOID CARNIVORES
OUTSIDE MANCHESTER GREGS PROTEST
VEGAN SAUSAGE ROLLS
ARE TO BE SOLD THEY DETEST
GREGS VEGGIE PASTIES
HAVE BEEN SOLD FOR YEARS
THEY TASTE THE BEST
THE CARNIVORES MUST BE WORRIED
ABOUT THE EUROPEANS INTEREST

31

THE JOURNEY OF LIFE
PEACE OF MIND
IS THE ULTIMATE FIND
FOR HUMAN KIND

32

IT TOOK TWO WORLD WARS
FOR THE WORLD TO UNITE
BUT IT ONLY TAKES ONE NEANDERTHAL MORON
TO TRUMP THE WORLDS CLIMATE CHANGE TREATY

33

HERE WE ARE AGAIN NEW YEARS EVE
CITIES AROUND THE WORLD SHOWING
AFFLUENCE 8 TONS OF GUNPOWDER
WHAT A WASTE
MAKING TITILLATING COLOURS OVER LONDON
GONE UP IN SMOKE
THE HOMELESS COULD HAVE BEEN HOUSED
SO EVERYONE WITH A PHONE MAKE ONES OWN
PRETTY COLOURS IN THE SKY BESPOKE

34

ONE NOTES THE QUOTE
THE CREAM SHALL ALWAYS FLOAT TO THE TOP
SO TOO THE TURDS DO THEY NOT

35

WE HUMANS DEFINE HUMANITY
WHETHER ONE SWEEPS THE ROAD
MAKES THE ROAD OR OWNS THE ROAD
ALL THE HUMAN TRAFFIC ON THE ROADS
OF KINGS EMPERORS AND ALL DICTATORS
AND PRESIDENTS ARE REPRESENTATIVE OF
OUR WORLD IN THE 21st CENTURY
CAUCASIANS HAVE NOT CHANGED MUCH
SINCE THE ROMAN TIMES
PERSECUTION OF BLACKS MUSLIMS AND JEWS
MURDER OF CHRIST TOO

INTRODUCING CURRENCY AND
ESTABLISHING THE CATHOLIC CHURCH
WITH ITS PENULTIMATE LEADER
THE POPE
THE BEGINNING OF WHITE SUPREMACY
AND HOW FAR THE MAFIA

36

WITHOUT WOMAN THERE IS NO MAN
MAN WITHOUT WOMAN THERES NO HUMAN
LIFES BIOLOGICAL AND BIOCHEMICAL BALANCE
WITH ALL THINGS LIVING DEPENDS ON MAN
TO CLEAN UP HIS ACT AND GIVE HALF THE WORLD BACK
TO WOMEN WHO WILL RE-EDUCATE MAN IN THE WAYS
FORWARD WITH LIFES NEW FACTS

37

ONE IS ANTI CHRISTIAN
ONE IS ANTI JEW
ONE IS ANTI ISLAMIC
ONE IS ANTI ANYONE
WHO HAS A RELIGIOUS VIEW
SECULARISM MAYBE
ATHEISM TOO

38

WHEN DOES ONES SELF RESPECT
DETERIORATE TO DISRESPECT
ANOTHER PERSONS
SPACE MIND AND BODY
DISREGARDING ONES CHOICE
AND ONES INTELLECT
HAVING NO SAY
TO REFLECT
ON PAST AND POST
HYPNOTIC SUGGESTIONS
MUST BREAK ALL HUMAN RIGHTS
LAWS OF THE UNITED NATIONS

39

HARD ON THE HEALS
FOOT TO THE FLOOR
CAN'T GET ANY SPEED
OUT OF THIS ANYMORE
ONE GETS OUT OF LIFE
WHATEVER ONE PUTS IN
LOVE OR LIES
PASSION OR DECEIT
HONESTY AND LOYALTY
COME HIGH ON THE LIST
WITH RESPECT AND DIGNITY
THAT COMES WITH A TWIST
ALL THIS AND MUCH MORE
COMES WITH A KISS
A KISS WITHOUT LOVE
IS IT WORTH ALL OF THIS

40

IGNORANCE OF ONES PARTY POLICIES
IS NO DEFENCE OF ONES NAIVE POLITICAL VIEW
THE POST APOCALYPTIC POLITICAL WALKING DEAD
THE INDEPENDENT MINDED Ltd Co OF THE SEVEN EGOS
WHOM ALL BECAME M Ps ON LABOURS MANIFESTO
ARE WHIPPING THEMSELVES AWAY FROM THE LABOUR PARTY

41

JOHN LENNON ATE THE APPLE
DREW WHAT HE SAW THEN
OPENED THE BEATLES APPLE STORE
IN LONDON 1967 BAKER St No 94

42

TO LEAVE ONES AMASSED FORTUNE
TO ONES CAT
TELLS ONE HAS NOT FOUND LOVE
LOYALTY AND TRUST IN ANOTHER
HUMAN BEING ON THE CONTRARY
ONE MUST HAVE DIED SAD AND
BITTER TOWARDS ONES
FELLOW MAN

43

TO MAKE LOVE WITH YOUR BEST FRIEND
THERE IS NO MORE TO COMPREHEND

44

IF MAN HAD SPENT THE SAME
AMOUNT OF TIME AND MONEY
ON CLEANING AND HEALING EARTH
AS MAN HAS DONE ON SPACE EXPLORATION
EARTH WOULD BE THE MOST WONDERFUL
AND PRECIOUS PLANET IN OUR UNIVERSE

45

WHO'S TELLING US THIS
WHO'S TELLING US THAT
WHO'S SELLING US SHIT
WHO'S SELLING US CRAP
WHO'S GETTING THIS AND
WHO'S GETTING WHAT
WHO'S STAYING IN AND
WHO IS NOT

46

TO BE RACIALLY DEFINED
AND SOCIALLY BLIND
IS TO THE DEPRIVATION
OF ALL HUMAN KIND

47

NUMBER NUMBER EVERYONE'S A NUMBER
YOUR A NUMBER I'M A NUMBER
EVERYTHING'S A NUMBER OF ZEROS AND ONES
NO ONES NUMBER ONE
JUST ONE OF OVER 8 BILLION
NOW THAT'S A NUMBER

48

PIONEERS CHALLENGE
FIRST THEY CHALLENGE THEMSELVES
THEN ULTIMATELY THEIR OBJECTIVE
DOCUMENTED JOURNEYS TO WHEREVER
TO LEARN BROADEN AND ENHANCE
ONES KNOWLEDGE AWARENESS
AND EXPERIENCE THE SPACE
BETWEEN PLANETS AND CONTINENTS
THE SPACE BETWEEN ATOMS
AND VEINS IN BRAINS
TO ADMINISTER DRUGS
IN THE HOPE TO MAINTAIN
COGNITIVE MOVEMENT IN HUNTINGTON' S DISEASE

OR PARKINSON'S DISEASE
GUINEA PIG PIONEERS
DESERVE OUR MOST HIGHEST GRATITUDE
C H E E R S

49

THE WORLD IS AWASH
WITH OUR WASTE
WINDING DOWN RIVERS
LYING ON RIVER BEDS
WASHED OUT TO SEA
FLOATING PLASTIC MAYBE
EATEN BY BIRD FISH AND MARINE
ALL FEEDING ON OUR PLASTIC DEBRIS

50

AUSTERITY DENIES
CHOICE OF WORK WAGES AND CAREER
CHOICE OF HOME ADDRESS AND LIFE STYLE
CHOICE OF FOOD FRIENDS AND CULTURE
CHOICE TO QUESTION
WHAT IS WRONG IN SOCIETY
CHOICE TO QUESTION
WHAT IS RIGHT IN SOCIETY
CHOICE TO QUESTION ONES FREEDOM

51

I AM NOT A WHISPERER
SILENT BACK HAND SPOKEN WORDS
WHISPER MISTER SINISTER SISTER
WHISPER NOT THE LIES THE PLOT
WHISPERERS SLEAZE BEHIND DO THEY NOT
WHISPERS MUST BE SEIZED UPON
THEN SPOKEN OUT LOUD
WHISPERERS ARE MUTTERERS OF
THE SILENT BACK HAND SPOKEN WORDS
TO JEST TO PEST TO SUGGEST AND REQUEST
THE LIES THE PLOT
WHISPERERS SLEAZE BEHIND DO THEY NOT
WHISPERS MUST BE SEIZED UPON
AND SPOKEN TO A CROWD
OF GATHERED FRIENDS AND PEERS
THEN MADE TO SPEAK OF THEM OUT LOUD

52

WOW IF WOMEN STOP WORKING
THE WORLD WOULD STOP TURNING
YES AND THE MEN
WOULD BE LEFT WONDERING HOW

53

DOES IT MATTER WHAT HEAD
ONES IS KICKING DOWN THE ROAD
DOES IT MATTER WHAT BODY

IT BELONGS TO ONE KNOWS
A HEAD ATTACHED TO A BODY
IS REALITY
DETACHED FROM A BODY
IT HAS NO ANATOMY
SO HOLD ONES HEAD UP
AS IF IT'S TO BE CHOPPED OFF
HEADS IT'S MINE
PICK IT OUT OF THE TROUGH
TELL THE TRUTH OWN THE CRIME
ONE CHOSE THIS PATH OF MURDER
DO THE TIME

54

WHEN DOES ONES IMPRESSION
BECOME ONES ASSESSMENT
WHEN DOES ONES ASSESSMENT
BECOME ONES THEORY
WHEN DOES ONES THEORY
BECOME ONES POINT OF VIEW
WHEN DOES ONES POINT OF VIEW
BECOME ONES CONVICTION
WHEN DOES ONES CONVICTION
BECOME ONES JUDGMENT
TO BE JUDGMENTAL

55

ONE KNOWS WHAT IT'S LIKE
WHEN ONE SHOOTS ONESELF IN THE FOOT
ONE KNOWS WHAT IT'S LIKE
WHEN ONE PUTS ONES OWN FOOT IN ONES MOUTH

ONE KNOWS WHAT IT'S LIKE
WHEN ONE BITES ONES OWN LIP
ONE KNOWS WHAT IT'S LIKE
WHEN ONE KNOWS ONES IN TOO DEEP
ONE KNOWS WHAT IT'S LIKE
WHEN ONE KNOWS ONES NOT A SHEEP
ONE KNOWS WHAT IT'S LIKE
WHEN ONE HAS TO LEAVE TO SLEEP

56

ONE MUST ACCEPT THE FACT
HUMANS NEED TO BREATHE
SO WE NEED CLEAN AIR
ONE MUST ACCEPT THE FACT
HUMANS NEED TO EAT
SO WE NEED HEALTHY FOOD
ONE MUST ACCEPT HEALTHY FOOD
NEEDS HEALTHY SOIL NO G M O
NO PESTICIDES NO GLYPHOSATE
HUMANS NEED CHOICE
SO NO INDOCTRINATIONS
BY RELIGION AND POLITICS
ONE MUST ACCEPT THE FACT
CHOICE IS OUR FREEDOM

57

SQUADRON OF SQUAD DRONES

58

GOD AND COUNTRIES
GONE ARE OUR TREES

59

WHEN TRUTH BECOMES A CONSENSUS
CONSENSUS LEAD TO CONCESSIONS
CONCESSIONS LEAD TO CRITERIA
CRITERIA LEAD TO CONDITIONS
CONDITIONS LEAD TO CORRUPT CULPABLE COMPENSATIONS
WITH THE OPPORTUNITY TO DRAW THE WRONG CONCLUSIONS

60

THE IMAGINARY WORLD EVERYONE LIVES IN
IMAGINING LIFE AS SOMEONE ELSE
IMAGINATION OF FRIENDS PAST AND FUTURE DEPEND
ON ONES PRESENT CREATIVE IMAGINARY IMOGI

61

CHARLTON HESTON'S IRON FIST CORPORATE
GANG OF GUN SELLING HAWKS
HAVE CHANGED EARTHS PLAYING FIELDS OF WHITE POPPIES
TO BATTLEFIELDS OF RED POPPIES
AS 50 FAMILIES MOURN THE DEATHS OF THEIR LOVED ONES
DOZENS MORE GRIEVE THEIR LIVES SHATTERED FOREVER
THE WHOLE OF NEW ZEALAND AUSTRALIA AND THE WORLD
ACKNOWLEDGE THE WHITE RIGHT TO BARE ARMS IS WRONG

62

ONES CHOICE ENDS
WHEN ONES DISEASE APPEARS
WITHOUT WARNING OR GRADUALLY
MAKING RANDOM APPEARANCES
AT DIFFERENT PLACES AND
LENGTHS OF TIME
PAINFUL OR NOT
DISRUPTIVE AND CHALLENGING
AS ONES NEW FRIEND MAYBE
ONES CHOICE OUR FREEDOM
SURRENDERS TO ONES DISEASE

63

THE GOOD THE BAD
THE HAPPY THE SAD
THE SMILES THE ANGER
THE LAUGHTER THE BANTER
SUGGESTIONS AND QUESTIONS
GESTURES AND PLEASURES
PRIVATE AND PERSONAL
DELETE THE GROOMING CREEP

64

DEPRESSION MAYBE
A LACK OF EMPATHY

65

BEING A WHITE CAUCASIAN
HOMO SAPIEN HUMAN
ONE MUST ACKNOWLEDGE
AND ACCEPT ONE IS CULPABLE
FOR ALL OUR ANCESTRAL
FATHERS COLONIAL PAST
FOREVER LANDSCAPING
CONQUERING DESTROYING
MINING INDOCTRINATING
AND BUILDING EMPIRES
ON THE BLOOD SWEAT TEARS
AND BONES OF OTHER ETHNIC
HUMAN BEINGS

66

THE COST OF THE CARBON FOOTPRINT MAY'S GOVERNMENT HAVE SPENT SQUANDERED AND WASTED ON HER DEFIANT AND DISMISSIVE RED LINED BACK STOP BREXIT IS WHOLLY AND UTTERLY BEYOND ALL THE COMPREHENSION OF OBSCENITY

67

AFTER BREXIT EXHAUSTION
BREXIT FATIGUE
THE BREXIT BURIAL
WILL BE WELCOMELY RECEIVED

68

MISTER PIG AND PIGLET
WHITE RABBIT AND MARCH HARE
LIZARD WITH PARROT
BLACKBIRDS WITH CATERPILLARS
BUTTERFLIES WITH FLAMINGOS
DORMOUSE WITH ELEPHANT
BOTH WISHING THEY WERE AS COLOURFUL
AS ALL THEIR EXQUISITE FRIENDS

69

THE GARDEN SPEAKS VOLUMES
WITHOUT PEOPLE WITHOUT WORDS
PEOPLE SPEAK VOLUMES
OF NONSENSE SO ABSURD
VOLUMES OF GARDENS
PEOPLES WITHOUT WORDS
NONSENSE SPOKEN
IN GARDENS EXPOSED

70

CAPITALISM
ORGANISED SELFISHNESS
DOES NOT WORK BECAUSE
CAPITALISTS DO NOT LIKE TO PAY THEIR TAXES

71

ROCKS AND MINERALS
AROUND NECKS ARE CRIMINAL

72

ONE STANDS ONE HEARS
ONE SEES THE TEARS
ONE FEELS THEIR PAIN
TEARS DOWN THE DRAIN
ONE CRIES ONE TRIES
TO DRY THEIR EYES
ONE FEARS THEIR SMILES
SHALL FOREVER DISAPPEAR
ONES FOCUSED ONES DETERMINED
ONE CAN CHANGE FEAR AND TEARS
WITH LOVE AND COMPASSION
AND EMPATHY MY DEARS

73

PEN AND PLECTRUM
BOOK AND GUITAR
THE ARTIST IN ONE AND OTHER
IS NEVER TOO FAR

74

SOCIETAL BREAKDOWN
COMMUNAL BREAKUP
POLITICAL BREAKDOWN
CAPITALISM FUCK UP

75

MAYS SEVEN HOUR CABINET MEETING
DISCUSSING BREXIT LEAVING
THEY ONLY CAME UP WITH ONE THING AGREEING
LETS BRING IN JEREMY CORBYN

76

BREXIT FLEXTENSION
U Ks AND E U s CONVERSATION

77

IT IS A CRIME AND
THE LAW OF THE LAND
TO HIDE ONES MONIES AND ASSETS
AWAY FROM THE CHANCELLOR MAN
THE TAX MAN OR ONE IS FINED
AND/OR IMPRISONED
SOVEREIGN QUEEN E II
HER PRIVILEGED FEW
BANKS AND CORPORATIONS
KEEP THEIRS OFF SHORE TOO
SETTING AN EXAMPLE
OF HOW NOT TO
PAY ONES TAXES AND
GET AWAY WITH IT THROUGH
TAXING THE WORKING CLASS
AND LETTING THEM BELIEVE
THEY HAVE A SAY TOO

78

ITS A TERRIBLE DAY AT THE RACES
WHEN EVERY FAVOURITE WINS
YES NOT FOR THE FEW BOOKMAKERS
WHEN THEY HEAR MANY A PUNDIT SING

79

THE ILLUSTRIOUS ILLUSTRATORS IMAGINATION
TO IMMACULATELY IMITATE THE IMPRESSION

80

IDEAS ARE BULLETPROOF IN LIFE AND
TO CONFIDE AND HAVE PURPOSE IN LOVE

81

ONE MAY LEAVE ONES FOOTPRINT IN THE SANDS OF TIME
BUT OH TO LEAVE ONES FOOTPRINT IN HUMANKIND

82

THE 21st CENTURIES FIRST
PROFOUND INNOCENT PIRATE OF PUBLISHING
JULIAN ASSANGE
THE EX EDITING CHIEF OF WIKILEAKS
THE WORLDS DIGITAL DICTIONARY OF
FACTS AND TRUTHS
ARRESTED AT THE ECUADORIAN
EMBASSY LONDON
AFTER ITS PRESIDENT BECAME
THE FIRST TO RESCIND ASYLUM

83

NOTRE DAME SPIRE
DESTROYED BY FIRE
FRANCE MOURNS NOT NECESSARILY
FOR ITS RELIGIOUS STRUCTURE
MORE FOR ITS ARCHITECTURE
AND ARTS FOR THE ARTISANS OF ALL PARISIANS
THE POPES ASSURANCES FROM ABOVE
SHALL COST THE WEALTHY NON TAX PAYING CATHOLIC CHURCH
TO PAY FOR ITS OWN INCREDIBLY EXPENSIVE REAL ESTATE IT SELF
AS THE FRENCH TAX PAYERS HAVE PAID AND PRAYED ENOUGH
UNLESS OF CAUSE GUILTY BILLIONAIRE SINNERS COUGH UP

84

ALL RELIGIONS STATE
THEY ARE AT THE HEART OF THE COMMUNITY
YET THEY ARE NOT IN THE SYSTEM
THEY DON'T PAY TAXES NOR INSURANCE DIVIDENDS
IT IS THEREFORE EXACTLY WHY THEY REPAIR THEIR OWN
OBSCENE REAL ESTATE PORTFOLIO ROOFS THEMSELVES
AS ACTS OF THEIR GOD ARE TRUELY EXPENSIVE
AS ALL WE HUMBLE HUMANS KNOW FAR TOO WELL
INSURANCE COMPANIES DO NOT PAY OUT FOR GODS TANTRUMS
ACTS OF GOD

85

THE SOVEREIGN FIRM FAMILY
KEEP THEIR WEALTH OFF SHORE
SO TOO THE BILLIONAIRES
AND THE GANG OF BLUES
IT IS WE POOR SUBJECTS
WHO WORK CREATE AND MAKE DO
THEY HAVE PROVED THEY ARE
CRAP AT MANAGEMENT
THEY CAN ALL STAY OFF SHORE
BE INDEPENDENT
HAVE A DEMOCRATIC PRESIDENT

86

MAN PUT A PRICE ON MINERALS
MAN PUT A PRICE ON ANIMALS
MAN HAS PUT A PRICE ON ALL LIVING LIFE NOW
MAN HAS PUT A PRICE ON MAN

87

ONE DOES NOT BELIEVE IN PRAYERS
AS ONE KNOWS EVERYONE PREYS ON ONE ANOTHER

88

DISCIPLINE ITSELF ACHIEVES NOTHING
DISCIPLINE THE MIND AND ACHIEVE ALL

89

ONE IS NOT AGAINST MAN IN THE RACE
ONE IS NOT AGAINST MACHINES IN THE RACE
ONE IS NOT AGAINST TIME IN THE RACE
ONE IS JUST BEING IN THE HUMAN RACE

90

ONE IS NOT A CITIZEN
OF THE SOVEREIGN ACT
ONE IS JUST A SUBJECT
SUBJECTED TO THE SOVEREIGNS TAX
IT IS THEREFORE CRIMINAL AND IN LAW
NOT TO PAY TAX IF ONE KEEPS ONES WEALTH OFF SHORE
FOLLOW HRH EXAMPLE OF THIS
AS BRITAIN STARES AT ITS FUTURES ABYSS

91

ONE FEELS LIKE AN ELEPHANT
IN THE LONG GRASS
EVERYONE TALKING ABOUT ONE
BEHIND ONES ARSE

92

PAINTERS AND POETS
PRODUCE IN PEACE
PRINTED AND PUBLISHED
BY SILENT ARTISTS

93

I DIDN'T HAVE TO SAY A WORD
MY MOUTH WAS OPEN
I MUST HAVE LOOKED ABSURD
GAPING AT ONE SO UNBELIEVABLY BEAUTIFUL
I PARDON MYSELF IF ONE THOUGHT ME TO BE RUDE
ON THE CONTRARY I AM POWERLESS
AS TO MY EMOTIONS AND VIRTUES
I MAYBE STRICKEN WITH LOVE
BY SUCH A BEAUTY AS YOU
HENCE HERE WITH THE WITNESS OF MY LOVE TO YOU
NOW WRITTEN IN INK MAY YOU SWEET BEAUTY LOVE ME TOO

94

IT MUST BE SO INDIGNANTLY SAD
FOR ALL THE OLD SOLDIERS OUT THERE
WITH NOTHING TO KILL EXCEPT TIME
PLEASE ACCEPT PEACE

95

ITS NOT WHETHER ITS
RIGHT OR WRONG
ITS THE MORAL OF THE DAY
THAT SINGS THE SONG
OF THE PRINCIPLE WAY
WE ALL GET ALONG

96

ONE TURNS UP
ONLY TO BE TURNED OVER
ONE TURNS ROUND
TO FIND ONES BEEN TURNED IN
IT TURNS OUT
ONES BEEN TURNED DOWN
SO ONE TURNS WITHIN
TO FINALLY TURN ONESELF ON
AND TURN THE CORNER
THEN TAKE ONES TURN
BEFORE ONE TURNS OFF

97

MOTHER WEEPS
TEARS FLOOD DOWN HER CHEEKS
SHE WILL CRY FOR WEEKS
GLAZED EYES NUMB AND WEAK
STILL UNABLE TO SPEAK
FOR TO DO SO SHE MIGHT HAVE TO ACCEPT MAYBE
THE LOSS OF HER LOVED ONE HER BEAUTIFUL BABY
THE GRIEF THE LOVE WITH NOWHERE TO GO
NOTHING NOBODY NO ONE NO BABY TO SHOW
GRIEFS JOURNEY LOVES JOURNEY EXISTS ONE KNOWS

98

A GLASS OF LEGAL
AN ARMY OF UNPAID VOLUNTEERS
SOME PEACE OUT OF NOTHING
MAY COME SOMETHING TO PLEASE
ACHIEVE ONES DENIAL
ACCOMPLISH OTHER DESIRES
PUZZLE WITHIN AND OUT
DISCIPLINE ONES FIRE

99

WHEN FATHER SAW SON
CRUCIFIED TO A CROSS
HE IMMEDIATELY KNEW
WHERE HIS 3 NAILS HAD GONE

100

CANAPÉS AND CHAMPAGNE
UNDER CANOPIES UNDER RAIN
KEEPING ALL AND SUNDRY DRY
GORGING ON ILL GOTTEN GAINS

101

P. PEOPLES FROM ALL PARTS OF THE WORLD
POSTING PROTESTS THESE ARE
E. EDUCATED ENTHUSIASTS ENTITLED
TO EXAMINE EXPLORE AND EXPLAIN
A. AS AN ARMY OF ACTIVISTS USING THEIR VOICE
TO ACTIVATE
C. CLIMATE CHANGE BY CONCERNED CHILDREN
WORLD WIDE CRYING C H A N G E
E. EARTHS ENERGIES

102

WOVEN WORDS WEAVE THEIR WISE OR WOES
WHERES WHENS WHYS AND WHAT FORS
WHETHER THEY'RE WAYS ARE WRITTEN OR WRONG
WORDS WILL BE SPUN SPOKEN WRITTEN OR SUNG

103

WALKING ON AIR
ONE DOES NOT CARE
ONE IS FLYING
WALKING ON SEA
ITS A BREEZE
ONE IS DREAMING
LIFES NO JOKE
ONE CAN'T COPE
ITS MISERY
LIVING ON BROKE
THERE SEEMS NO HOPE
ONES AFLOAT
ONES HOMELESS
ADRIFT AT SEA

104

CHUMPS AGAINST ROBOTS
ALGORITHMS RULE
FACELESS DATA SUBJECTS
BAR CODED AND NOTED
PROCESSED TO BE VIEWED

105

CALF HORMONE GROWTH FEED SHAKE
THROWN AT FARAGE A CRIME
DOES ONE AND ALL FORGET
CORBYN'S FACE WAS A MILITARY TARGET

106

NAIVE OR IGNORANT
BIGOT OR ARROGANT
BELGIUM DOCTORS NEED
AN EDUCATED HAND
STATING JAIL TIME
SHOULD BE SERVED TO PARENTS
WHO BRING THEIR CHILDREN UP
TO BE VEGAN

107

THREAD BARE CLOTHES
RIPPED AND TORN
LAYERS OF COLOURED
MATERIAL WORN
TIGHT LEGGINGS AND DENIM
T SHIRTS AND TRAINERS
THE SWEAT SHOP CLOTHING
IS SMOTHERING MOTHER NATURE

108

TO FIND LOVE
FALL IN LOVE
THEN LIVE WITH LOVE
AND FRIENDSHIP WITH
SOMEONE DOING ONES WASHING
AFTER ONE HAS WASHED THEIR HAIR AND
COOKED AND CARED FOR EACH OTHER IS
LOVE WITH UNCONDITIONAL BENEFITS

109

K R E M L I M TRUST
NEEDS VERIFICATION

110

LEAVE IT
LEAVE OFF
LEAVE IT ALONE
LEAVE IT OUT
LEAVE IS WITHDRAW
LEAVE IS NOT IN
LEAVE IS EXIT
LEAVE IS OUT

111

IT IS A SAD TIME TO WITNESS
THE FIRST TWO DECADES OF THE 21st CENTURY
SUBJECTED TO DEPLORABLE DIPLOMATIC
POLITICAL PERSECUTION OF POOR PEOPLES HUMAN RIGHTS
GIVING BIRTH TO THE MANY THOUSANDS OF FOOD BANKS NEEDED
WHILST THE FEW RECEIVE OBSCENE FINANCIAL REWARDS

112

BLIND IGNORANT BIGOTRY
IS TO THE DEPRIVATION
OF ALL IN THE HOUSE
OF ALL IN THE FAMILY
OF ALL IN THE NEIGHBOURHOOD
OF ALL IN THE COMMUNITY
OF ALL IN SOCIETY
OF ALL IN THE COUNTRY
OF ALL IN OUR WORLD

113

IGNORANCE OF THE DRUG LAWS
IS NO EXCUSE OR DEFENCE
IGNORANCE OF DRUGS
IS NO EXCUSE OR DEFENCE
OF THE BLIND IGNORANCE AND BIGOTRY
APPLIED TO THE CHOICE AND HEALTH FACTS
OF ALL LEGAL TO BE LEGAL AND NON LEGAL DRUGS
WHICH ARE ALL PLANT BASED BUT THEN
SYNTHESISED BY PHARMACEUTICAL THUGS

114

ONES HEAD IS FULL OF SHIT WRECKS
SHIT WRECKS OF LIFE
NIGHTS AND DAYS FULL OF SHIT
SHIT DAYS AND SHIT NIGHTS
SHIT WRECKS IN ONES MEMORY
SHIT WRECKS OF ONES LOVE LIFE
SHIT WRECKS LEFT ADRIFT
LEFT FLOATING OUT OF SIGHT

115

CRY YOUR ART OUT
LET IT OUT
JUST GET YOUR ART OUT THERE
LET YOUR ART SHOUT

116

ARE WE ALL EACH AND EVERY ONE OF US
ARE WE ALL PREPARED TO MASSIVELY DISOBEY
DEMAND OUR WORLD LEADERS TO MAKE
RADICAL CHANGES TO OUR WORLDS CLIMATE TODAY

117

CHARLES DARWIN TURNS IN HIS GRAVE
AND JULIAN ASSANGE RATTLES HIS CAGE
AS ECUADOR GIVES RIGHTS TO U S A
TO BUILD AIR BASE ON GALAPAGOS ISLANDS TODAY
THE FINAL NAIL IN EARTHS FRAGILE ECOSYSTEM
M A N HAS F A I L E D

118

I LEAVE MY LIFES WORK
MY ART WORLDS OBSERVATIONS
PEOPLES WORTH PLANET EARTH
WORDS WORTH CONVERSATIONS

119

TICK TICK
TIME IS TICKING
FASTER AND FASTER
NO MORE EXCUSES STOP KIDDING
NO PLASTIC PLASTERS
FOR FUTURE CLIMATE DISASTERS
USE THE TIME LEFT OWN IT
SURPASS CLIMATE CHANGE LIMIT

120

WHERE IS TOCK
WHERE HAS TOCK GONE
TIME KEEPS TICKING
WITHOUT TOCK ALONG
TIMES FIRST TICK
WAS TIMES FIRST TOCK
ONE NEVER HEARD A TICK
NOT FOLLOWED BY A TOCK
MANS FIRST TIME WAS NATURALLY
TIMES GRANDFATHER CALLED CLOCK
NOT A GRANDFATHER CLICK
BUT A GRANDFATHER CLOCK
SO TOCK IS COMMENDED
FOR ALL TIME AS A CLOCK
WHILST TIME KEEPS TICKING
THERE ARE NO CLOCKS
BUT WATCH
WATCHES WORN AROUND WRISTS
SO ONE CAN WATCH TIME IN JUST A TWIST
TIME IS SILENT VISUAL DIGITAL DATA
NO TOCK NO TICK

121

EVEN WHEN EQUALITY MEANS
NO DISCRIMINATION OF GENDER
WOMEN MUST BE RESPECTED
THEIR DIGNITY PERSONIFIED

122

MAPLE LEAVES ARE PROBABLY BETTER USED
WIPING CANADIAN ARSE HOLES
RATHER THAN CHOPPING DOWN
THE LUNGS OF CANADAS TREES

123

RELIGIONS HYPOCRISY
IS HUMANITIES MALIGNANCY
RELIGIOUS BELIEFS
HYPOCRITICAL THIEFS
RELIGIONS USE FEAR AS
LOVE OF A GOD THAT DOES NOT EXIST
PROVE IT
HYPOCRITES

124

APATHY OF ACCEPTANCE
ANGER AT ALL ADDRESSES
APARTHEID POLITICS
ADDRESS THE APATHETIC ANGER
AND APPEASE ALL PARLIAMENTARIANS

125

WHILST THE WORLD EMBRACES
AND FORGES INTO THE FUTURE
WITH ELECTRIC AUTOMOBILES
HOW DOES ONE ELECTRIFY
THE WORLDS WORK HORSE
THE WORLDS TRACTORS
THE WORLDS MAIN POLLUTING
DIESEL TRACTION MOBILE MACHINES

126

TODAY IS A NICE DREAM DAY
NICE DREAMS ALL ROUND
WHILST ONE PLAYS AND CREATES
ONE MEANS TO CAPTURE IT SEEMS
ON PAPER CANVAS VEGETABLE
MINERAL DIGITAL SCREENS
ONES ODYSSEY OF ART
EXISTS IN ONES OWN DREAMS

127

I AM GLAD IT HAS TAKEN ME MY WHOLE LIFE
TO GET TO WHERE I AM
WITH DEATH AROUND ANY CORNER MY FRIEND
I WRITE BOOKS SONGS AND POETRY WITH A HEARTY PEN

128

THE ENEMY IS MEDIOCRACY
LIVE LIFE EMBRACE DEATH

129

BLIND ACCEPTANCE OF FAITH AND FACTS
IS WITHOUT KNOWLEDGE EXPERIENCE AND WISDOM TO DOUBT
THE ESTABLISHED SYSTEM UNDER WHICH WE ARE ALL CHAINED
SO WITHOUT QUESTIONS WITHOUT CHALLENGE THERE IS NO
CHANGE

130

ONE BELIEVES BIRDS
ARE INTO BREAD

131

BIRTHDAYS ARE FUN WHEN YOU ARE 5
BIRTHDAYS ARE EXCITING WHEN YOU ARE 10
BIRTHDAYS ARE SPECIAL IN YOUR TEENS
BIRTHDAYS ARE FACT IN YOUR 20s
BIRTHDAYS ARE A MATTER OF FACT IN YOUR 30s
BIRTHDAYS BECOME VAGUE IN YOUR 40s
BIRTHDAYS ARE ABSURD IN YOUR 50s
BIRTHDAYS ARE EVEN FORGOTTEN IN YOUR 60s
BIRTHDAYS BECOME REMARKABLE IN YOUR 70s

BIRTHDAYS ARE INCREDIBLE IN YOUR 80s
BIRTHDAYS ARE WONDERFUL IN YOUR 90s
BUT WHEN YOU REACH 100 OR MORE
YOUR JUST BLOODY MARVELLOUS THATS FOR SURE

132

INDIAS CHESS PIECES ARE SPREAD
EVENLY AROUND THE GLOBE
TO BE PLAYED TO BE CHALLENGED
TO BE GIVEN THE CHANCE TO GLOW

133

MUSIC TO MY EARS IS THE WRITTEN WORD
SUBTLETY SPOKEN WITH DIALECT AND DICTION
SUNG LOUDLY OR QUIETLY WITH ACTION AND CONVICTION
BUT MOST DEFINITELY WITH CHARACTER LOVE AND COMPASSION
ALL THE WORLDS WRITTEN WORDS ARE SURLY THERE TO BE READ
TO BE HEARD

134

ONE FOOT AND ONE CONSONANT
IN FRONT OF EACH OTHER
BEGINS A JOURNEY
TO WHEREVER ENDS
FOOT STEPS INTO STRIDES
CONSONANTS SPELL WORDS
MARCH ON FORWARDS
SENTENCES ABSURD

UNLESS MEANING TRUTH
FACTS PREFERRED
LOVE LIES UNDER TRUTH
HATRED BREEDS BENEATH AND
THROUGH THE TANGLED WEEDS
THAT LIES GREW TO TARNISH
THE WORLD OPAQUE YET PURE
TO MAKE CLEAR AND TRANSPARENT
THE MURKY WORLD WE VIEW
THAT ALL IS HUMANLY RIGHT
THAT ALL IS HUMANLY TRUE

135

WHY DOES THE WORLD MAKE OIL
IT IS USED TO LUBRICATE
MAYBE THE CONTINENTAL PLATES
OIL IS USED AS A COOLANT
MAYBE TO COOL OCEANS AND PLANTS
THIS OIL IS ALSO A FOSSIL ENERGY FUEL
TOXICALLY OVER USED BY IGNORANT HUMAN MULES
THE FOOLS

136

BAN BANNON
BARON OF BILLIONAIRE BIGOTS
CAPITALIST CLOWNS CONCERNED ONLY TO
CASH IN ON THE CLIMATE C H A N G E

137

DEVINE PROVIDENCE
DESCRIBE DEVINE PROVIDENCE IN
THE U S A LAND OF HOPE AND
SPIRALLING OUT OF CONTROL DREAMS

138

COMPETITION IS THE ESSENCE OF GAMBLING
THE TOOL OF DIVISION IN POLITICS
THE SYSTEM THAT SERVES RELIGIONS
BY SEPARATION AND DISTRACTIONS AND
THE FUNDAMENTAL NATURE OF SOVEREIGNS
TO RULE WITH COMPETITIVE PASSIVE LAWS
KEEPING THEIR SOCIETY ON THE BRINK OF WARS

139

AMERICAN BALL
AMERICAN HAND BALL
AMERICAN THROWING BALL
AMERICAN CATCHING BALL
AMERICAN CRADLING BALL
AGAINST ONES CHEST
AND THEN LAUNCHING
BALL WITH ONES
WHOLE BODY LEAPING
THROUGH THE AIR
DOES NOT IN ANYWAY
CLARIFY ELUCIDATE NOR EXPLAIN

THE USE OF THE WORD FOOT
IN RELATION TO THE AMERICAN TITLE OF A BALL GAME
AMERICAN HAND THROWING CATCHING CRADLING BALL PERHAPS
BUT WHATS A FOOT
SAID A MAN ONCE WIELDING A SHAKING SPEAR

140

THROUGH PRINTED WORD
AND PAINTED CANVAS
MAY THEIR ART CAPTURE
AND ILLUMINATE REALITY

141

THE SOVEREIGNS BLUE BLOOD
IS OF THE DEADS FLOWING BLUE
SPILT SLAUGHTERED AND SHED
IN THE NAME OF KING THEN COUNTRY
BUT WHAT OF YOU

142

ALL FOR ONE AND ONE FOR ALL
FRENCH AND ENGLISH SOCIALIST WALK TALL

143

SOW A SEED
GROW A TREE
CONTEMPLATE THE TREE
GROWING AND SHEDDING LEAVES
BRANCHES OUT IN OUR ATMOSPHERE
SIMPLE SILENT GROWTH APPEARS
SEASONAL RAINS AND SUNLIGHT EACH YEAR
NURTURES ITS LIFE TO LIVE AND BE HERE

144

WHEN SONS DESTROY
THEIR MOTHERS h e A R T
THEY KNOW NOT WHAT THEY DO
FORGIVE THEM
N O T

145

ONE MUST BE REMINDED
MAN MUST NEVER FORGET
RUSSIANS MURDERED LITHUANIAN
JEWS IN THEIR DEATH CAMPS

146

THE LIES THE PLOTS
OF THE POPULOUS LOT
LOBBYING CAPITALIST
BILLIONAIRE BIGOTS
THEY HATE THE POOR
YET NEED THEM FOR SURE
KNOWING THEY ARE THE CATALYST OF LIFE
THEY WON'T LET THEM VOTE SOCIALIST NO MORE

147

THE UNIQUENESS OF A TREE
IS AS UNIQUE AS YOU OR ME

148

BOOKS AND BONSAIS
AND CANVAS COLLIDE
THERE WHERE MUSIC
AND POETRY RESIDE
PICTURES CAPTURE DECADES
OF FASHION AND HAIRSTYLES
TO BLACK AND WHITE PHOTOGRAPHS
OF AFRICAS WILD 1 9 6 8

149

NATURE
NURTURE
NATURAL

150

AFTER AUSTERITY
ACCEPTANCE OF APATHY
WITH ACCOUNTABILITY
WE CAN AFFORD E M P A T H Y

151

I AM ACCOUNTABLE FOR THE WORDS IN MY SONG
THE WORDS IN MY POETRY EXPLAIN WHATS GOING ON
I AM NOT ACCOUNTABLE FOR AUSTERITY
ACCEPTANCE OF APATHY OR ABUSE ALLOWED TO BE USED FREELY
I AM ACCOUNTABLE FOR MY HUMOUR MY BEHAVIOUR MY DRESS
SENSE AND MANNERS OR NOT AS ONE EXPERIENCES
I AM NOT ACCOUNTABLE FOR THIS PUPLIC ABUSE FROM LANDS
END TO JOHN O GROATS FROM PICCADILLY TO LONDONDERRY
ABUSE ALLOWED TO FESTER
IN THE MORAL HIGH GROUND EXPENSIVE NAME OF REGIONAL AND
CENTRAL POWERHOUSE CONSERVATIVE PARTY CONTROL

152

HERE WE GO AGAIN
BOJO AND DOH DOH
MEDIA ECCENTRICS ACCENT STAKE
DOING THEIR ATLANTIC DOUBLE TRICK DOUBLE TAKE

153

WELCOME WONDERS WE WISH
TO SPEAK THE LETTERS ARRANGED AS WORDS
DESCRIBING ONES FEELINGS AND MESSAGE
FACT FRANTIC FICTITIOUS FALSE OR
SILENTLY QUIVERING THE BREATH OF A SONGBIRD
TO OBSERVE SURVEY STUDY AND TAKE IN
THE ARTISTS CREATION AND TO COMPREHEND
WHAT ONE SEES WHAT ONE LIKES INSTANTLY
WHAT ONE LOVES ABOUT THIS PIECE
MAYBE IT IS JUST THAT
THE ARTIST HAS CAPTURED
P E A C E

154

FROM THE END OF THE FOREWORD
AND FROM THE TIP OF MY PEN
I SHALL ENDEAVOUR TO CAPTURE MY OBSERVATIONS
FOR ONE AND ALL TO COMPREHEND

155

WANDERING TO WORK STEPPING OVER
SOON TO BE DEAD HOMELESS PEOPLE
WONDERING WHAT WEALTH IS TO BE MADE
COME WHAT MAY
ONE MIGHT BE READING SHAKESPEARE OR DICKENS
NO THIS IS THE 21st CENTURY BRITAIN TODAY

156

OBSERVATIONS OF TRANSITIONS IN GENDER VEGETARIANISM
SOCIALISM AND SECULARISM IN THE TWENTY FIRST CENTURY
WITH EDUCATED DETERMINATION PASSION HUMOUR AND EMPATHY
FOR ONE AND ALL IN LIFES JOURNEY FOR LOVE AND PEACE

157

Dr AMA The F L O S S O P H E R

158

DO NOT TAKE PRISONERS
TAKE PRIDE IN THE PASSION OF ONES WORDS
PARTICULARLY PIN POINTED
PREFERABLY PERSONALISED
FOR PEOPLES PROFOUNDLY PERSONIFIED
PERHAPS PERMANENTLY
PERHAPS PARTIALLY

PERHAPS PRESENTLY PART TIME
POST P45s AND C Vs
FOOD BANK TOKENS AND VOUCHERS
FROM POST CODE LOTTERY

159

THEY EVEN ARGUED IN HARMONY
THE BEE GEES BROTHERS GIBB

160

LIKE BONSAI TREES
DEPRIVATION OF PEOPLES
DEVELOP STRENGTHS CHARACTER
AND BEAUTY WITHIN THEMSELVES

161

DARE BRING TO BARE
BEAUTY TO SHARE
FROM ONES HORIZON
TO ONES PALM IN HAND
A BREATH OF AIR
SEEDS ROOTS LIFE FORM TO CARE
FOR ITS LIFE STYLE CHARACTER
ITS ESSENCE CHERISHED
LIKE CHAMELEONS THROUGH SEASONS
LEAVES COLOURS CHANGES
AND WHEN NEW BUDS FORM
OLD LEAVES WILL FALL

AS ONE AND ALL TAKE A REST
TAKE STOCK AND SIGH
LOOKING AT THE UNBELIEVABLE
BEAUTY OF A BONSAI

162

THE SMELL THE STENCH
OF DEAD LIFE BEING COOKED
BLOODY FLESH AND LIMBS
TO TEAR NIBBLE AND CHEW

163

TALK TO ME WONT YOU
TALK TO ME SOMEONE
TALK A LOAD OF COCK
TALK A LOAD OF BOLLOCKS
TALK ABOUT ANYONE
TALK ABOUT ANYTHING
TALK YOUR TALK
TALK YOUR WORDS LET THEM SHOUT
TALK CONVERSE USING WORDS
SOCIAL BLINDNESS LEAVES OUT

164

ONLY FOOLHARDY PEOPLE ARE TAKEN IN
BY THIS HOCUS POCUS IN PARLIAMENT

165

SOME PEOPLE WANT TO BE AN AUTHOR A WRITER
OTHERS JUST WANT TO WRITE BOOKS

166

TWO PIECES OF BONE
DICED INTO CUBES
1 THROUGH TO 6
INSCRIBED TO VIEW
THE CUBES ARE CALLED ROCKS
WHEN THROWN WERE ROLLS
JUST LIKE THAT OLD MUSIC
DICE ROCKED AND ROLLED

167

ONE I AM AGAINST
MURDER OF ANY KIND
HUMAN MAMMAL
FISH BIRD AND ANIMAL
STOP KILLING WILD LIFE

168

STARS ARE LEFT OVER
PIECES OF LIGHT
CRYSTALS OF ENERGY
OLD AND BRIGHT

169

LOVERS OF THE DAY
BECOME LOVERS OF THE NIGHT
LOVERS THAT RESPECT EACH OTHER
WHETHER THEY'RE THERE OR NOT
LOVE MAY COME RARELY OR PURELY
TRULY LOVE CAN RAIN A LOT
NOT KNOWING LOVE AT ALL
MUST SURLY BREAK ONES HEART

170

DISCIPLINE YOURSELF TO TAKE CONTROL
OWN ONES CHOICE TO MOTIVATE MANAGE OR EVEN
CHANGE AN ASPECT OF ONES LIFE
THE ACHIEVEMENT DISCIPLINE GIVES ONESELF
IS THAT YOU ARE A WINNER
USING ONES OWN DISCIPLINE WILL POWER

171

SUN SHINES LIKE LAZER BLADES OF LIGHT
PIERCING DOWN THROUGH THE GREY BLACK CLOUDS
THUNDER BOLT THEN A LIGHTNING STRIKE
ITS THE MIDDLE OF THE DAY
IT FEELS LIKE THE MIDDLE OF THE NIGHT
HALE STONES THUNDEROUSLY FALL FROM THE SKY
A DELUGE OF WATER RAIN AND MUD SLIDES
TORRENTIAL WEATHER AND MONSOON WILL TAKE LIVES
WHETHER INSECTS OR BIRDS ANIMALS OR HUMANS
LIFE IS FRAGILE AS ONE AND ALL EXIST TO SURVIVE

172

MOTIONLESS SUSPENDED
SPACIAL EMPTINESS
NO MATTER
MUSIC FLOATS EVERYWHERE
WAVES OF DRIFTING NOTES
ORCHESTRALLY GATHER
THEN PART ALONE
AS MAY MUSICS MAGIC MINSTRELS PLAY
FOR SHIPS IN THE NIGHT
AND STARS THROUGH THE DAY

173

A JOURNEY TO
A JOURNEY FROM
A JOURNEY TO WHEREVER
A JOURNEY TO FIND A LOVING HOME

174

WHETHER ONE HAS OR HAS NOT
WHETHER ONE HAS BEEN
A HAS BEEN AND FORGOT
WE ALL END UP DEAD DO WE NOT

175

JEREMY CORBYN AND JULIAN ASSANGE
ONLY HAVE WORDS NOT BLOOD ON THEIR HANDS

176

THE BLIND APATHY OF DENIAL AND ACCEPTANCE
OF THIS SYSTEM OF FEAR AND CRUELTY
ANIMALS REARED AND SLAUGHTERED
NEVER SEEING DAYLIGHT

177

LATELY
ONE FEELS EVERYBODY HATES SEE
THEY DON'T GET TO FEEL FREE
THEY'RE NOT ABLE TO GET TO BE
FREE OF AUSTERITY
LATELY
NO ONE SEES EYE TO EYE SEE
KEEP EVERYBODY BEGGING PLEASE
ACCEPTING THE PITTANCE FROM AUSTERITY
LATELY
ANIMALS REARED AND SLAUGHTERED
NEVER SEEING DAYLIGHT WHAT BREED
RAPE REARED MEATS WASHED DOWN WITH
CALF HORMONE GROWTH FEED
LATELY
NATIONALISM AND RACISM ONE SEES
DIVISIVELY BREATHE THEIR BREATH TO LEAVE
BRITAIN A BANANA REPUBLIC TAX HAVEN
EATING CHLORINE MEATS AND G M O FOODS
WITH A LOW WAGE WORK FORCE MOST PROBABLY
LATELY
ELEPHANTS ARE ALL ONE SEES
NO ONE ELSE SEEMS TO SEE THEM
EXCEPT PEOPLE LIKE ME
SOCIAL ELEPHANT BLINDNESS IS A DISEASE
POLITICALLY ALGORITHM FED BY AUSTERITY
THE FINANCIAL STRAIGHT JACKET FRAUD BUT LEGAL SEE

178

PHYSICAL DISEASE
IS EASIER TO SEE
THAN MENTAL DISEASE
EMPHASISING MORE EMPATHY PLEASE

179

COLD WINTERS LOST UNDER SNOW
WHITE FLAKES OF CRYSTALS UNIQUELY FLOATING
THEN SETTLING ONE KNOWS
SPRING IS AROUND THE CORNER
WHATEVER THE WEATHER WILL TURN FINE
BUDS AND BULBS AND TUBULARS ALL SPRING TO LIFE
SPROUTING AND SHOOTING AND DISPLAYING LEAVES
BRINGING FORTH THE COLOURS OF THEIR FLOWERS TO BE
A GASP AT THEIR BEAUTY THEIR EXQUISITE ARRAY
BEFORE AUTUMN ARRIVES BEARING DEATHS SYTHE
LEAVES NOW GOLDEN YELLOW AND REDS
FALLING AS THEY MAY TO THEIR GRAVES TO THEIR BEDS

180

FEAR DEATH SUSPENSE AND SUBTERFUGE
SERVE ALL IN PARLIAMENT
THE POLITICIANS AND THE RELIGIONS
AND ARE GOOD ALL ROUND MEDIA ENTERTAINMENT

181

SLAVERY WAS SO CALLED ABOLISHED
OVER 200 yrs AGO
WHITE COLONIALISTS WERE NOT BY LAW
TO BUY OR SELL BLACK NEGROES
HOW SAD AND IRONIC THE SLAVE TRADE HAS EXISTED
NOW CALLED HUMAN TRAFFICKING ON THE CONTINENT OF AFRICA
MEN WOMEN AND CHILDREN ALL BOUGHT AND SOLD
MAINLY BY BLACK AFRICAN ISLAMIC TERRORISTS
BUT YOU CANNOT CALL THEM NEGROES

182

FISH LIVING IN A CAGE
UNDER WATER IN A LOCH
BEING EATEN ALIVE BY LICE
HOW GROTESQUE
WHO ARE THESE
LOCH NESS MONSTERS

183

LIFE THROUGH A LENS
USED TO BE PHOTOGRAPHY
NOW LIFE IS SEEN TOTALLY
THROUGH A LENS   ALIENS

184

LOOK BEYOND THE BOOK
ONE IS READING

185

CARBON FOOTPRINT DRIFTS
IN SANDS OF TIME

186

ONES NEXT STEP IS VITAL
TO ONES OWN DEAR FUTURE

187

WE ARE ALL BLACK SHADOWS
DARK IN THE LIGHT
SHADOWS IN THE NIGHT
OUT OF SIGHT

188

DEMOCRACY DIES AS QUEEN E II WRITES
ON THE 28th AUGUST 2019 HER OWN EPITAPH
THE UNELECTED ELIZABETH II BECOMING
BRITAINS WORST AND MOST UNDEMOCRATIC
REINING MONARCH PROROGUING PARLIAMENT
FOR UNELECTED (EXCEPT FOR A FEW TORIES)
P M JOHNSON TO GET ALL HIS
PUPPETS AND PUPPETEERS
PERSUADING AND BULLYING ALL TO VOTE
AND BECOME BRITISH BREXITEERS

189

THE FUTURE IS NOT GOD
IT IS G A F A T
GOOGLE APPLE FACEBOOK AMAZON TWITTER

190

THIS IS THE TRUTH
THIS IS THE BIS
SETTLEMENTS MADE IN SWITZERLAND 1930
STRANGELY APPEARED BEFORE HITLER BECAME CHANCELLOR
AND FRANCO NEEDING THE CHANCELLORS HELP
AND THEN THE SECOND WORLD WAR
WELL WELBA (ROTHSCHILD)ROSS TRUMPS AID AND
DOMINIC CUMMINGS BEING JOHNSONS AID WITH
MACRONS FAMILY IN FRANCE
ALL HAVE THEIR SETTLEMENTS
NOT BY CHANCE

191

MUSIC FOR THE SOLES
OF ONES DANCING FEET

192

PEOPLE ARE FOOD BLIND
FOOD BLIND FOR WHAT THEY EAT
BLIND TO THE FACTS
THEY EAT PAINFUL ANIMALS MEATS

193

SUBMIT ONESELF TO A HIGHER POWER
ONE SUBMITS ONESELF TO SUBORDINATION

194

WHEN A RAT
IS ISOLATED FROM THE PACK
THE RAT BECOMES LONELY
DEPRESSED AND SAD
WHEN ISOLATED RATS ARE ALLOWED
TO GATHER WITH OTHER ISOLATED RATS
AT THE SAME TIME OFFERING THEM
WATER OR OPIATED WATER
EVENTUALLY ALL RATS DRANK OPIATED WATER

WHEN OPIATED WATER WAS INTRODUCED
TO A NORMAL RAT FAMILY CIRCLE
THE OPIATED WATER WAS ONLY SNIFFED AT

195

IT IS EASY TO NOTICE
THE SELFISH CAPITALIST BUT DON'T ASK
THEY ARE THE ONES WITH THEIR NOSE IN THE AIR
WITH NOTES OF THEIR QUEEN UP THEIR ARSE

196

FROM BRITAIN TO HONG KONG
FROM AMERICA TO RUSSIA
FROM SAUDI ARABIA TO AFGHANISTAN
DEMOCRACY IN OUR WORLD IS THREATENED

197

G WHIZZ GUYS
200 SATELLITES IN THE SKY
NO ONE IS GOING TO FRY
IT IS JUST 5 G L I V E

198

HEALTHY EATING LIKE FRESH FRUIT AND VEGETABLES
PEOPLE LIKE VEGANS AND RAW FOOD EATERS
ARE NOW REGARDED AS AN EATING DISORDER
OBVIOUSLY BY PASTORAL FARMERS

199

CAN YOU IMAGINE THE WAY I FELT
BEING WHIPPED WITH A LEATHER BELT
WITH THE LASHING WHIPPING STINGING AND WELTS
AS I TURNED AND GRABBED HIS BOLLOCKS TO SEE
HIS ANGER MELT DOWN AS HE KNELT
AND CRIED OUT HIS GRIEF FROM THE HAND HE WAS DELT

200

SEPTEMBER 2019
ALL IS NOT WELL IN BRITAINS BREXIT WORLD
NOW IS THE TIME TO NAIL ONES COLOURED SALES
TO THE MASTer OF DEMOCRACY

201

THE MONSTROUS CHEMICAL CORPS OF MONSANTO
THEIR GLYPHOSATE NOW SOWN WITH THEIR G M Os
THOUSANDS OF PEOPLE HAVE DIED
AND 10s OF THOUSANDS MORE WILL ONE KNOWS

NOW PURDUE LIKE MONSANTO IS FOUND GUILTY FOR THE U S As
OPIOID OVERFLOW
100s OF THOUSANDS MORE DEATHS WILL FOLLOW
THE HIDEOUS GROTESQUE SHAREHOLDERS OF PURDUE & MONSANTO

202

WITH SWORDS DRAWN AND PENS OUT
ITS TIME FOR COURAGE IN BREXIT'S LAST BOUT
KENNETH CLARKE THE CONSERVATIVE GRANDFATHER
OF THE HOUSE
BACKS JEREMY CORBYN AS INTERIM P M NO DOUBT
NICOLA STURGEON 1st MINISTER OF SCOTLAND AND
MARK DRAKEFORD 1st MINISTER OF WALES BOTH JOIN THE ROUTE
TO BRING DEMOCRACY BACK TO PARLIAMENT
INSTEAD OF PROROGATION BY THE QUEEN
AND ALL BEING LEFT OUT

203

DOMENIC CUMMINGS BREXIT AID TO UNELECTED P M BORIS
BULLYING BRITAIN WITH QUEENS PROROGATION BLUFF
BRITAIN DEMANDS DEMOCRACY
BRITISH PEOPLES HAVE HAD ENOUGH

204

PRUDENCE DIPLOMACY AND COURAGE
SERVES ONE WELL AT ANY AGE

205

A SMILE EXPRESSES
MANY THINGS
MOST IMPORTANTLY LOVE
HAPPINESS HOPE AND DREAMS

206

H R H PRINCE ANDREW AND THE 17yr OLD VIRGINIA
SHALL FOREVER BE REMEMBERED WITH EPSTEIN
THE AMERICAN CHILD MOLESTER BILLIONAIRE
WHO EVIDENTLY TOOK HIS OWN LIFE IN PRISON OUT THERE

207

SEPTEMBER 4th 2019
DEMOCRACY RETURNS TO HONG KONG
ITS CITIZENS UNANIMOUSLY PROTESTED
TO TAME ITS NEIGHBOURS DRAGON
THE PROPOSED EXTRADITION BILL WITHDRAWN
BY CHIEF EXECUTIVE CARRIE LAM

208

THE TRUTH IS IN THE CLASSROOM
FROM A SOCIALLY MINDED INTERRELATIONSHIP
CONNECTIVITY SHARING CLASSROOM
TO A INTER BRED INTO THEMSELVES

OLD ROYAL ESTABLISHMENT LED SET OF RULES
FOR THE PRIVILEGED OFFSPRING OF THE
MILLIONAIRE AND BILLIONAIRE BIGOTS AND BRUTES

209

THE CUMMINGS OF BORIS JOHNSONS BREXIT
BANNERS POSTERS AND BILLBOARDS BOASTING
BRITISH BULLDOG BORIS BEST
YES TO BANKRUPT BRITAIN SELL THE N H S AND
IMPORT G M O AND CHLORINE CHICKEN FOR THE POOR
AND THEN PISS ON EVERYONE ELSE

210

THE POUND TOOK A DIVE
WHEN BORIS IN No 10 ARRIVED
AND WITH 1st GLIMPSE OF CORBYN IN No 10
THE POUND STARTS TO RISE

211

BREXIT HAS BROUGHT OUT
THE WORST AND THE BEST
IN POLITICS POLITICIANS AND MEDIA
ESPECIALLY WHEN BORIS INVOLVES THE QUEEN
FOR PROROGATION OF PARLIAMENT
A WASTE OF PRICELESS DEBATING TIME
AND MAYBE ILLEGAL
IN THE EYES OF MOST IT SEEMS

212

WHEN HAS IGNORANCE
EVER SOLVED ANYTHING
IGNORANCE WILL NOT
SOLVE OR STOP BREXIT

213

THE CROWN ONLY PROVES
BY DEFAULT OF OTHERS HEADS
THE CROWN RULES WITH NO OPPOSITION
PARLIAMENT MAYBE USED TO DEFUSE ALL OPPRESSION

214

A BURLINGTON BUGGER OF A PRIME MINISTER BORIS
CALLING HIS Rt Hon OPPOSITION A CHLORINATED CHICKEN
WHEN THE Rt Hon GENTLEMAN IS A RENOWNED VEGETARIAN
IS NOT ONLY INSULTINGLY ABHORRENT
IT IS ARROGANTLY MADE PLAIN AND CLEAR TO ALL THAT
THE PRIME MINISTER IS IGNORANT

215

COINCIDENTAL BORIS THE BEEFEATER
FUNDS MORE TO SCOTTISH FARMERS
AS THE QUEEN PREPARES BALMORAL
FOR BORIS AND GIRLFRIEND FOR HIGH TEA
A LITTLE PAY BACK FOR HRH
DON'T MENTION ANDREW GET DOWN ON YOUR KNEES

216

FROM THE GRASSROOTS OF EVERY C L P
CONSTITUENCY LABOUR PARTY MEMBER
GATHERING MOMENTUM ON THE WAY
WITH PUBLIC SUPPORT FOR LABOURS
N E C NATION EXECUTIVE COUNCIL TO
ENDORSE AND BACK THEIR LEADER J C
JEREMY CORBYN TO PLAY A COMPLETE
BLINDER IN THE PARLIAMENTARY SYSTEM
OF VOTES IN BOTH HOUSES TO PASS A
LAW PROHIBITING A NO DEAL BREXIT AND
FORCING THE CONSERVATIVE PARTY WHOM
UNANIMOUSLY VOTED THEIR BIG WHITE
HOPE OF A BREXITEER P M BORIS JOHNSON
TO GO CAP IN HAND TO BRUSSELS AND
ASK FOR AN EXTENSION TO ARTICLE 50 TILL
Jan 31st 2020 OR GO STRAIGHT TO JAIL

217

ANEURIN NYE BEVAN GAVE US THE N H S
HE HELPED TO KEEP THE H BOMB IN 1958
WITHIN A MONTH C N D WAS BORN WITH
MICHAEL FOOT M P
BERTRAND RUSSELL PHILOSOPHER
J B PRIESTLEY AUTHOR
AND JAMES CAMERON JOURNALIST FORMED
A MARCH FROM LONDON TO ALDERMASTON
THE CAMPAIGN FOR NUCLEAR DISARMAMENT
WAS ALIVE AND WELL ESTABLISHED BY THEM

218

THE FACTS STACK UP WE CAN ERADICATE POVERTY
AND HOMELESSNESS FOR LESS THAN 1% G D P
PER COUNTRY ONCE AND THE POSITIVE BENEFITS
SHALL BE 5 TIMES GREATER THAN SPENDING
THE SAME AMOUNT EACH YEAR ON BOMBS

219

THE CHILDREN AND GRANDCHILDREN TO BE
BORN IN OUR POLLUTED OVER POPULATED
SELFISH SOCIETY ON A ONCE BEAUTIFUL
NOW EXHAUSTED WEATHER DRYING PLANET
SHOULD SERIOUSLY BE THOUGHT OF

220

2019 AND ONE IS HIT WITH THE LACK OF INSECTS
FLYING CRAWLING WRIGGLING OR SQUIRMING
THE SOUND ALONE IS DEAFENING QUIETER LIKE
THE EROSION OF OUR SEA GRASSES AND CORALS
GHOSTLY SILENT WITH NO VISITING GUESTS

221

AS WITH THE DEATH OF CORAL REEFS
BY OUR OWN MAKING THE NEWS
PAPER FROM FORESTS OF TREES
SAWN DOWN FOR ALL TO READ
IS TOXICALLY SHAMEFUL
AND OBSCENELY HYPOCRITICAL
GO DIGITAL
AND ACKNOWLEDGE AND BE
CLIMATE CHANGE WISE AND FREE
OF NEWS PAPER FORESTS OF TREES

222

THEY KNOW WHO THEY ARE
THE ONES WHO PERSUADED
BOUGHT BULLIED BANKROLLED
OR BANKRUPTED WESTMINSTER
CAREERS BY THE BANKERS
THE WANKERS THE BILLIONAIRE THIEVES
CORPORATE AND MEDIA MOGULS
WE DO NOT NEED

THESE ARE THE PEOPLE WHOSE
ONLY MOTIVATION IN LIFE IS GREED
OF MONEY OF POWER OF BREXIT
THEY ARE ALL CULPABLE
DOES ONE CONCEDE

223

BORIS JOHNSONS CUMMINGS AND
GOINGS OF CABINET MINISTERS
AND MEMBERS OF PARLIAMENT ARE
THE SHORT CUMMINGS OF BREXIT ADVICE

224

SELFISH MEATHEAD BULLYS
NOT ONLY THINK THEY ARE RIGHT
THEY NOT ONLY BELIEVE THEY ARE RIGHT
THE BIGOTS ALL KNOW THEY ARE RIGHT WING FASCISTS

225

FREDDIE McCONNELL
MOTHER SO STRONG
SPEAKS AND DELIVERS
FOR ALL TRANSGENDERS
TAKE COURAGE
LOVES WHERE YOU BELONG

226

YES DAVID WALLACE WELLS
THE WORLD IS FULL OF HAWKS
FUCKING AND RAPING EARTH
THESE PRIVILEGED FASCIST CUNTS
WHOS ONLY GOALS IN LIFE ARE WEALTH
HAVE FUCKED THE SOCIALIST POOR
FOR FAR TOO LONG CREATING
THE TITLE OF YOUR BOOK
THE UNINHABITABLE EARTH

227

LOVE IS MORE THAN A TENDER KISS
BRUTAL HONESTY HUMOROUS LOYALTY
COURAGE AND INTEGRITY
SHALL PROVE ALL THIS

228

WHO WOULD HAVE THOUGHT
TOM PORGY WATSON
WOULD HAVE SHRUNK
SO LOW
AGAINST HIS LEADER
AGAINST HIS PARTY
AGAIN IT IS
THE TOM WATSON SHOW

229

START ONES CONVERSATION
ONE KNOWS ITS THERAPY
ITS WHEN CONVERSATIONS STOP
ONES VULNERABILITY IS IN JEOPARDY

230

CAMERON AND BORIS'S
BURLINGTON BOYS
GARDEN OF EATON
SERPENT TOYS

231

A MESSAGE IN A BOTTLE
SAYS IT ALL
BOTTLING IT UP SOLVES NOTHING
SPEAK TO SOMEONE CONVERSE JUST CALL

232

ONE SPEAKS AND WRITES
WITH A SOCIALISTS TONGUE
NO FAIR-WEATHER WORDS
WILL BE WRITTEN WRONG
WORDS WILL WIELD
THEIR WRITE-FULL WAY
WHERE EARS WILL HEAR TRUTH
WRITTEN AND SPOKEN
AS SOCIALISTS SAY

233

YOU ARE MORE THAN
THE SUM YOU ARE
TO ME YOU SUM UP
ALL IN OUR LIFE
ALL IN OUR DREAMS
YOU ARE SO MUCH
MORE THAN YOUR SUM
TO ME YOU ARE
THE SUM OF MY LIFE
THE SUM OF MY LOVE
I KNOW WHAT
YOU GIVE TO ME
LOVE

234

AN OCEAN OF SAND
A DESERT SEA
ESCHER'S STAIRS
BACK FROM FRONT
FORWARD PAST
MEMORIES ETCHED
STONE FIRE GLOWS
HAMMER BLOWS
STEAL THE NIGHT SHOWS

235

IT IS NOT WISE TO WIPE
ONES FEET ON THOSE
WHO PAVED THE WAY FOR
OTHERS SUCH AS ONESELF

236

EVER SINCE THE FIRST WORLD WARS
PROPAGANDA MACHINE STARTED
EVERY GOVERNMENT NEWSPAPER
RADIO T V MEDIA CORPORATION
HAVE BURIED LIES AND TRUTH
WITH FAKE AND REALITY
PLUNGING THE WORLD WITH ITS
GREEDY INCONSIDERATE INHABITANTS
INTO ITS FOSSIL TOXIC FUELLED
POLLUTED FUTURE BY BURNING
THE MIDNIGHT OIL

237

YES ONE SEES FEWER BIRDS
YES ONE SEES FEWER FLIES
YES ONE SEES FEWER INSECTS
DOES ONE WONDER AS TO WHY
MAYBE ITS GLYPHOSATE
AND ALL PESTICIDES
OR MAYBE ITS WE LAZY GREEDY
SELFISH HUMAN BEINGS
LOOKING AND VOTING THE OTHER WAY
TURNING A BLIND EYE

238

THE BEE
OR NOT THE BEE
THIS IS LIFES QUESTION

239

ROCKS AND STONES
FASHIONED TO BLING
HILARIOUSLY UNFLATTERING
SHINING ON THE OUTSIDE
YET COLD TO TOUCH
AND WITHIN

240

JEREMY CORBYN HAS STEERED LABOUR
THROUGH THE BREXIT BLACK HOLE
WITH HIS STEELY EYE FIXED FIRMLY AND
DEMOCRATICALLY ON A PUBLIC VOTE
THE PEOPLES VOTE ASKING THE U K IF
A 2nd REFERENDUM ON BREXIT IS NEEDED
IN OR OUT YES OR NO

241

THE HARD OF HEARINGS
ADJOURNED FOR DINNER
THE PASTOR STOOD THEN
SAT SAYING THE FOOD IS
GOOD ENOUGH TO EAT
AN OLD GENTLEMAN ASKED
WHAT DID HE SAY
THE PASTAS GOOD
THE WOMAN NEXT TO HIM
ASKED WHAT DID HE SAY
THERES PARCELS FOR YOU
THE WOMANS HUSBAND
INQUIRES WHAT WAS SAID
ARSE HOLES TO YOU

242

CHANGE YOUR LIVES
CHANGE YOUR MINDS
CHANGE YOUR TIES
CHANGE YOUR LIES
CHANGE YOUR WAYS
CHANGE YOUR DAYS
CHANGE YOUR NIGHTS
CHANGE IS ALRIGHT
CHANGE YOUR MOOD
CHANGE YOUR FOOD
CHANGE YOUR NAME
CHANGE YOUR GAME
CHANGE YOUR SHOES
CHANGE YOUR VIEWS
CHANGE YOUR PLANS
CHANGE YOU CAN
CHANGE YOUR LIPS
CHANGE YOUR TITS
CHANGE YOUR HIPS
CHANGE YOUR BITS
CHANGE YOUR EYES
CHANGE YOUR SIZE
CHANGE YOUR WEIGHT
CHANGE YOUR MATE
CHANGE YOUR MOTHER
CHANGE YOUR FATHER
CHANGE YOUR SISTER
CHANGE YOUR BROTHER
CHANGE YOUR UNCLE
CHANGE YOUR AUNT
CHANGE YOUR FAMILY
CHANGE YOUR COUNTRY
CHANGE YOUR CONSCIENCE
YOU KNOW IT MAKES SENSE

TIME IS OF THE ESSENCE
FOR ALL PRIMATES
CHANGE THE CLIMATE

243

CONSCIOUS ACCOUNTABILITY
IS NEEDED FOR CLIMATE CHANGE
ACCOUNTABILITY FOR ONES ACTIONS
ACCOUNTABILITY OF GOVERNMENT SANCTIONS
ON CLIMATE CHANGE REDUCTIONS

244

CLIMATE EXCHANGE MONEY FOR LIFE
WEALTH GREED OF MONIES
IS THE VULGAR HUMAN PLAGUE
THAT IS FUELLING CLIMATE CHANGE
DICTATORS WITH EGOS OF BIGOTRY
BIAS AND IGNORANCE
CORPORATIONS BANKS BUSINESSES
AND THE MAN ON THE STREET WITH
THEIR BLIND ARROGANCE HAVE
BROUGHT US ALL TO OUR KNEES
AT THIS POINT AND PLACE IN TIME
WITH THE PLIGHT OF THE BEES
CLIMATE EXCHANGE FOR L I F E

245

WE HAVE ALL CRAWLED OUT
OF SOME CLOSET OR GUTTER
THE CULPRITS TOO UP THERE
IN THEIR CLOISTERED IVORY TOWERS

246

QUESTION THE SYSTEM OF ACCEPTANCE
WE ARE ALL BORN INTO
THAT WE ARE ALL BROUGHT UP
HETEROSEXUAL
THAT YOUR PARENTS OR PARENT
BRING YOU UP WITH
THEIR RELIGIOUS CHOICE OF BOOK OR
BOOKS ON SPIRITUALISM OR SECULARISM
THAT YOUR FATHER OR MOTHER
MAY BEAT YOU
THAT YOUR FATHER OR MOTHER MAY HAVE
EXTRA SEXUAL RELATIONS WITH YOU
THAT ANY ALL OR OTHER BLIND BIGOTRY
BELIEFS SHOULD BE TAUGHT BY PARENTS
EDUCATED BY TEACHERS IS THE
P R I M E E V I L C H E R R Y OF T R U T H
THAT THE SYSTEM IS B R O K E
CLIMATE CHANGE IS NO J O K E
AS EARTH C H O K E S Q U E S T I O N

247

W A T(SON) OF A TIME
FOR OLD CENTRALIST LABOUR
P M MILIBAND AND WAR CRIMES
P M BLAIR TO REAR THEIR HEADS
BEFORE CONFERENCE BRIGHTON
2019 TO STIR THE ALREADY MURKY
MUDDY WATERS OF BREXIT AND
ANTISEMITIC SWATHS OF CENTRALISED
CAPITALISTS CONCLUSIONS

248

FROM THE GARDEN OF EATON
AND THE HARROWING HILLS
THE OXBRIDGE DEBATERS
HAVE AT THEIR HEALS
THE ISLINGTON BYSTANDER
SEES AND HEARS ALL EQUAL
JEREMY CORBYN SPEAKS
THE LANGUAGE HOPES AND
FEARS OF ALL THE PEOPLE

249

THE POSTER READS
S P E E D K I L L S
L I E S T O O
MAKE WAR CRIMINALS

250

THE HOMO SAPIEN HUMANS
BEING THE WORLDS MOST
POWERFUL INHABITANTS
AND TOXIC DESTROYERS OF
LIFE MAN MUST SURLY NOW
REPAIR REPAY AND REBUILD
BANNING ALL FOSSIL FUELS
ONLY USING RENEWABLES

251

DIGITALLY DUMPED
TODAYS DEAR DIARY DELETERS OF DATA DATES

252

F 1
F O S S I L   1
RACING FUEL
NUMBER 1 FOSSIL FUEL

253

JOHN McDONNELL HAS A PLAN
A CENTRAL SOCIAL BANK FOR BRITAIN
FULL TRADE UNIONS WILL BE BACK
1 MILLION COUNCIL HOUSES BUILT
NO ONE TO WORK FOR THEIR POVERTY
PEOPLE ARE RIGHT TO ASK FOR 2nd REFERENDUM
NOW THEY KNOW THE FACTS TRUTH AND REALITY
OF LEAVING THE E U WITH A NO DEAL
ALL WORKERS SHALL HAVE A STAKE IN COMPANY
32 HOUR WEEK WITH NO LOSS OF PAY EVENTUALLY
A NON CARBON GREEN FUTURE WITH
INTERNATIONAL SOCIALISM BEING CULTIVATED
TO WORK WITH SOUTHERN POOR COUNTRIES
WITH GREEN TECHNOLOGY
AND WHEN ASKED IN THE FUTURE
WHERE WERE YOU WHEN
PEOPLE WERE LIVING OFF FOOD BANKS
PEOPLE WORKED FOR THEIR POVERTY
PEOPLE LAY DYING ON OUR STREETS
WHEN CLIMATE CHANGE THREATENED
ALL LIFE ON EARTH
ONE CAN SAY
ONE CONSCIOUSLY VOTED LABOUR
ONE BECAME A LABOUR MEMBER
AND LIVED TO HELP CHANGE
NOT ONLY THE CLIMATE BUT ATTITUDES
OF RACE SOCIALISM HEALTH HOUSING
FINANCE TAXATION AND ACCOUNTABILITY
TO CARE FOR ALL LIFE HUMANITY AND EARTH

254

24/09/2019
SUPREME COURT JUDGEMENT
FINDS PROROGATION OF PARLIAMENT
UNLAWFUL NULL AND VOID
THE PRIME MINISTER NEGLECTED HIS DUTIES
ASKING THE QUEEN WAS UNLAWFUL
AND PARLIAMENT WILL RESUME
11am 25/09/2019

255

ALL THOSE CONSERVATIVES MEMBERS
WHO SELECTED BOJO AS TORY LEADER
ARE ALL CULPABLE FOR THEIR ACTIONS
AND THE P Ms UNLAWFUL ACTIONS

256

WRITING READING AND PROGRAMMING CODE
IN THE 20th CENTURY IS COMPARABLE TO
THE READING AND WRITING
IN THE 18th AND 19th CENTURY
LETTERS COULD HAVE BEEN PRINTED ON
THE FRONT OF PUBLISHED NEWSPAPERS
ON BILLBOARDS AND POSTERS AND MOST
WOULD NOT HAVE BEEN ANY THE WISER

257

BORIS JOHNSON EPITOMISES
THE CONSERVATIVE TORY PARTIES
TOTAL DISREGARD OF THE SUPREME
COURT JUDGEMENT UNLAWFULLY
ADVISING THE SOVEREIGN QUEEN
AND THEIR ARROGANT ABUSE OF
THE OPPOSITION AND THE PEOPLE
BOTH OPPOSITION AND THE PUBLIC
NOW KNOW THAT THE CONSERVATIVES
ONLY BELIEVE IN ONE THING
WEALTH IS BEST FOR THEIR HEALTH
WITH NO HUMILITY CONCERN NOR
EMPATHY FOR THE PUBLICS HEALTH
THE POOR THE ELDERLY AND THE
DISABLED AND HOMELESS DYING ON
OUR STREETS THROUGH THEIR PROUD
AUSTERITY LEAVING 4 MILLION PEOPLE
IN THE 5th LARGEST ECONOMY ON THE
PLANET IN POVERTY ACCORDING TO
THE UNITED NATIONS NEW YORK

258

RUSSIAN SCIENTISTS MAKE BREAKTHROUGH
WITH MICRO CARBON EATING ORGANISMS
ABLE TO EAT ARTIC OIL AT -40 DEGREES
INDUSTRIAL GLOBAL USE WILL BE IN 2 YEARS
HOPEFULLY

259

THE WORST RHETORICAL LANGUAGE USED
IN PARLIAMENT FOR MANY DECADES PAST
WAS BLATANTLY USED BY THE ATTORNEY
GENERAL AND THE PRIME MINISTER WITH
INFLAMMATORY ABUSE HUFF AND THUNDER
AND HUMILIATION KNOWING THEY HAD GIVEN
UNLAWFUL ADVICE TO H R H THE QUEEN
AND WITH THE PRIME MINISTERS
PROTAGONIST WINSTON CHURCHILL'S
DO OR DIE POLITICAL POLICY THAT
SUCCESS CONSISTS OF GOING FROM
FAILURE TO FAILURE WITHOUT LOSS
OF ENTHUSIASM
THERE LEAVES NO HOPE OR CHANCE
FOR CHANGE OR APOLOGY FROM TORIES

260

NO ONE TRUSTS ANYONE IN THE HOUSE
NO PARTY TRUSTS ANY OTHER PARTY IN PARLIAMENT
NO ONE TRUSTS ANYONE IN GOVERNMENT MORE SO
THAN THEIR LEADER AND P M BOJO JOHNSON

261

A LOOPHOLE HERE
A PROROGATION WHEN AND WHERE
OR A LETTER TO ENGAGE
ARTICLE 50 BEFORE NOVEMBER

262

JESS PHILLIPS PIG BARREL POLITICS
HAS ONLY REVEALED HER TRUE COLOURS
AND HER PARLIAMENTARY EXPENSE ACCOUNTS
PAID FOR BY THE TAX PAYING PUBLIC

263

WHERE DOES ONE GO FROM HERE
WE CHOSE TO GO IT ALONE ONE FEARS
ONES FUTURES ARE NOT STABLE OR CLEAR
AS THE NATION HOLDS THEIR BREATH
HOLDING HANDS HOLDING BACK TEARS

264

Mr COLONEL SAUNDERS K F C
PAID A MISS CHILDRESS $1200 FOR RECIPE
IN TODAYS PRICE MISS CHILDRESS IS WORTH $20 000 WHOOPEE
COMPARE THAT TO $15 BILLION FOR Mr COLONEL SAUNDERS K F C

265

GRETA THUNBERG'S RHETORIC
ON ONE OF HER CLIMATE CHANGE BOUTS
HER PRIVILEGED OPPONENTS COMPARED HER TO
AN INTERNATIONAL CLIMATE CHANGE RELIGIOUS CULT
BEWARE OF THE POPULOUS RIGHT WAY
OF TURNING THINGS OVER ROUND AND ABOUT
THE CLIMATE MAN MADE FACES EXTINCTION
IS UNEQUIVOCALLY UNDER THREAT
THIS FROM THE SCIENTISTS AND PEOPLE LIVING IN EXTREME
THE CLIMATE NEEDS TO CHANGE THAT THERE IS NO DOUBT

266

THE AUTOCRACY BEING CREATED
AT THIS MOMENT OF TIME IN HISTORY
SHALL BE THE DEPRIVATION OF DEMOCRACY
AND THE DEMISE OF ALL LIFE ON EARTH

267

SPONTANEOUS ACCEPTANCE OF HAPPINESS
IN AFRICAN SCHOOLS ONE HAS WITNESSED
COMPARABLE TO WESTERN SCHOOL SYSTEMS
SPONTANEOUS ACCEPTANCE OF HAPPINESS
DOES NOT SEEM TO BE ALLOWED TO EXIST

268

Oh Yah Oh Yah
Oh DEAR ODEY
WHO BETS OR NOT
HE GETS HIS LOT
Oh Yah Oh Yah
Oh DEAR CRISPIN ODEY

269

WHATEVER HAPPENED TO JULIANNE ASSANGE
22 HOURS A DAY CONFINED ALONE
ARBITRARILY HELD IN THE UNITED KINGDOM
ONLY ONE 2 HOUR VISIT PER MONTH ALLOWED
EVERY JOURNALIST AND EVERY PUBLISHER
WRITER AND SPEAKERS OF FREE SPEECH
IN THE WORLD IS ON TRIAL HERE AND NOW
BRITAIN HAS NO PROOF THE U N AGREE
EXTRADITION TO AMERICA IS A NO NO
SET JULIANNE ASSANGE FREE

270

HAS ONE EVER HEARD OF
A HUMAN RIGHTS LAWYER
DEFENDING A BRITISH SOLDIER

271

AN L A BAG LADY
O MIO BABBINO CARO
FILMED SINGING OPERA
BY AN L A COPPER
IT WENT VIRAL
FLASH CROWD RAISED MONEY
FOR HER SURVIVAL
AND A MUSIC CONTRACT
FOR HER TO SING
THE MELODIES OF LOVE
TRAGEDY AND PASSIONS WITHIN

272

REFUSING TO APPEAR IN APRIL 2019
BEFORE A SELECT PARLIAMENTARY COMMITTEE AND
TO BE FOUND TO ADVISE THE P M TO PROROGUE
PARLIAMENT INVOLVING HRH THE QUEEN UNLAWFULLY
HAS RAISED ALARMS IN PARLIAMENT AND DOWNING STREET
OF DOMINIC CUMMINGS AND GOINGS PARLIAMENTARY PASS
6 MONTHS ON IN THE 2nd WEEK OF OCTOBER 2019

273

SURLY ONE IS NOT ALONE
IN FEELING THE BITTERNESS
AWAY FROM ONES HOME
THE BULLY BOY BURLINGTON BORIS
IS PROUDLY BELIEVED
WHILST JEREMY CORBYN IS
DISINGENUOUSLY SNEEZED
THIS SYSMIC SYSTEM OF
CHARACTER ASSASSINATION AND DOUBT
WHEN LIES BECOME TRUE
AND THE TRUTH BURIED SOME HOW

274

HOW CAN AN INDEPENDENT REPORT ABOUT
SCOTLAND YARDS INVESTIGATIONS INTO
THE METROPOLITAN POLICES HANDLING OF
THE FABRICATED CLAIMS THAT THERE WAS A V I P
PAEDOPHILE RING IN WESTMINSTER BE CREDITABLE
WHEN BACK IN 2002 PRIME MINISTER
TONY CHARLES MIRANDA LINTON BLAIR
CULPABLY LOCKED THE METROPOLITAN
POLICES INVESTIGATIONS INTO THE
WESTMINSTERS V I P PAEDOPHILE RING
AWAY FOR 100 YEARS AS TOP SECRET
SO HOW MUCH TAX PAYERS MONEY HAS BEEN POCKETED
BY THE ESTABLISHMENTS JUDICIARY LAWYERS AND THE
WASTED CIRCUS TIME SPENT ON AND BY THE REPORTERS
THE JUDGES LAWYERS POLICE AND REPORTERS
SHOULD ALL HAVE KNOWN THE FARCE THEY WERE REPORTING

275

HONG KONGS CHIEF EXECUTIVE MINISTER
CARRIE LAM
HAS UNITED HER CITIZENS EVEN STRONGER
AGAINST HER FACIAL MASKS BAN

276

COORDINATION AND TRANSFORMATION
RECYCLING THE WORLDS PLASTIC REGENERATION

277

PEACEFUL DEMONSTRATIONS
HAS ALWAYS BEEN THE PROTESTERS WILL
WHO WANTS TO GET BEATEN UP THREATENED
ARRESTED OR EVEN KILLED
2 MILLION VOICES FALL ON DEAF EARS
BLIND AS CARRIE LAM IS
WITH ALL OUR FEARS
SHE WILL NOT TALK OR DISCUSS
INSTEAD WE ARE PEPPER SPRAYED
WITH INDUSTRIAL TEAR GAS

278

1850s AMERICA
BROUGHT THE WORLD
F 1
FOSSIL FUEL No 1 OIL
THE 1920s EUROPE
BROUGHT THE WORLD
INTO THE PETROCHEMICAL AGE
FERTILISERS PESTICIDES AND OTHER BESIDES
THE 1940s 2nd WORLD WAR
BROUGHT INTO OUR WORLD
NUCLEAR BOMBS AND ENERGY
SO FOR OVER 150 YEARS
HUMANS HAVE DUMPED MILLIONS OF
METRIC TONS OF TOXIC CHEMICAL WASTE
INTO OUR ATMOSPHERE WHILST
RAPING AND BURNING EARTH OF HER
OTHER FOSSIL FUEL TREES
AND THE VEGETATION AND MINERALS MINED
AT AN ALARMING E X T I N C T I O N A B L E RATE
FOR THE LOVE OF BEEF AND OTHER ANIMALS TO EAT
INEVITABLY POISONING NOT ONLY THE AIR THAT WE ALL BREATHE
THE LAND DRAINING THE CHEMICALS INTO OUR STREAMS AND SEAS
WHERE CORAL FISH AND MARINE LIFE DIE IN FRONT OF OUR EYES
AND WITH OUR PRECIOUS DRINKING WATER ON A PERILOUS SLIDE
IN OUR ATMOSPHERE ONE WONDERS WILL WE BE ABLE TO SUR-
VIVE
DISCIPLINED DECISIONS TO DRASTICALLY DECARBONISE

279

ONE DOES NOT EAT ANIMALS
ONE LOVES THEM YOU SEE
JUST LIKE THE BIRDS
AND THE FISH IN THE SEA
ONE DOES NOT WANT TO KILL
ANY LIVING CREATURE THAT IS FREE
TO WALK TO BREATHE
TO SWIM IN OUR WATERS AND SEAS

280

WHAT DOES IT TAKE
FOR A POLICE MAN OR WOMAN TO AWAKE
WHEN AN 81 YEAR OLD LADY
IS ARRESTED NOT BY MISTAKE
WHEN THAT SYSTEM THEY UPHOLD
REPRESSES NOT ONLY THEMSELVES
BUT THE PROTESTERS (THEY FACE) FATE
276 EXTINCTION REBELLION CAMPAIGNERS FOR CLIMATE CHANGE
ARRESTED IN LONDON TODAY THE 7th OF OCTOBER 2019
WE STAND TOGETHER IN SOLIDARITY AND RESPECT
AS TODAYS CLIMATE CHANGE SUFFRAGETTES

281

THE WARRIORS OF TODAY
DO NOT NEED SHIPS OR ARMOURY
THEY ARE BORN IN THE 21st CENTURY
WELL EDUCATED WITH SMART PHONES AND UMBRELLAS
THEY PROTEST PEACEFULLY ALONG SIDE 80+ YEAR OLD HIPPIES
WHO ARE ALL DEMANDING CLIMATE CHANGE TO ZERO EMISSIONS

282

ALL HUMANS ON EARTH
SHOULD BE ASHAMED OF THEMSELVES
NOT HOLDING THEIR GOVERNMENTS TO ACCOUNT
FOR POISONING OUR WATERS STREAMS AND SEAS
POLLUTING OUR ATMOSPHERE BY SPRAYING
ATRAZINE BAYTHOID X L BICEP 11 MAGNUM
PHOSTOXIN LANNATE CORAGEN AND
MANY OTHER LETHAL CHEMICALS ONTO OUR FIELDS
AROUND HOSPITALS AND SCHOOLS URBAN AND RURAL
TO SAVE TIME
TIME IS MONEY
MONEY IS WEALTH
GOVERNMENTS AND CORPORATIONS HAVE PROVED
BY THEIR PAST IGNORANCE AND BLATANT OVER USE
AND MISUSE OF CHEMICALS THAT THEIR ATTITUDE IS
NO CONCERN NO COMPASSION OR CONSIDERATION
FOR YOUNG INFANTS CHILDREN AND YOUTHS BRAINS
AND THEIR HEALTH
NOW IS THE TIME FOR THE WHOLE WORLD TO MASSIVELY PROTEST
LISTEN CHANGE OUR CLIMATE IMMEDIATELY STOP THE MADNESS

283

WORDS GET IN THE WAY
WHEN ONE TRIES TO SPEAK
ONE IS ON A CLIFF EDGE BALANCING
A TECHNIQUE ONE HAS MASTERED AND IS AT ONES PEAK
WITH LETTERS PLAYING MUSICAL CHAIRS
ONE WONDERS HOW ONE GETS TO BE THERE
ARRANGING THE CONSONANTS IN AN ORDER TO READ
BUT TO MAKE SENSE OF THEIR MEANINGS
MAYBE A TRIFLE SUREAL
WHILE LINES OF WORDS
RIPPLE LIKE SNAKES ON WHITE SANDS
THE INK DRIPS FROM THE LETTERS
FORMING POOLS THEN RIVERS OF BLACK
BLANK MEMORY WHILE DISTANT CALLS ONE BACK
AS REALITY CHECKS IN
RAIN CHECK
BREATHE
DRINK WATER WET LIPS
SMILE THEN READ YOUR SPEECH

284

AFTER ALL THAT HAS BEEN SAID AND DONE
FROM THE CLASSROOMS AND BOARDROOMS TO GOVERNMENTS
STOP FRACKING BURNING FOSSIL FUELS
DECARBONISE INDUSTRIAL STEEL MOTOR ENERGY AND AGRICULTURE
THEN ONE WOULD BE DECARBONISING THE CITIES AND TOWNS TOO
HYDROGENATE OR ELECTRIFY THE WORKHORSES
THE TRACTORS AND TRUCKS AND ONE HALVES THE WORLDS
BACKBONE POLLUTER OR MORE IN ONE DECARBONISING DECISION

285

IT IS AS TRUE TODAY
AS IT WAS BACK THEN
IN THE 60s WE HIPPIES
READ THE WHOLE EARTH CATALOGUE MY FRIENDS
WE TOLD THE WORLD
STOP BURNING FOSSIL FUELS
STOP CHOPPING AND BURNING TREES
STOP DRINKING ALCOHOL
STOP EATING ANIMALS
STOP SMOKING TOBACCO
TRY SMOKING WEED
THE TRUTH HAS ALWAYS BEEN OUT THERE
IT IS ONES CHOICE TO LISTEN
TO BEND ONES EAR IS ONES WISDOM
TO COMPREHEND AND MAKE DECISIONS
ONE NEEDS TO HEAR ALL SIDES FACTS AND SOLUTIONS
WITH ALL THAT HAS BEEN SAID AND SPOKEN OF
NOW IS THE TIME TO HOLD ALL GOVERNMENTS TO ACT
CUT THE CARBON
CUT THE CRAP

286

I SEE FIRE I SEE LIGHT
I FEEL RAIN I FEEL PAIN
I HEAR THUNDER I HEAR CLAPS
I SHOUT SHIT I SHIT CRAP
I WALK ON THE SWEAT AND TOIL
OF MEN WOMEN AND KIDS
I WALK ON THE BLOOD SPILT
BY MEN WOMEN AND KIDS

I WALK ON THE TEARS SHED
BY MEN WOMEN AND THEIR KIDS
SO THAT THE LIKES OF I AND OTHERS AFTER
MAY SURLY BE HAPPY AND LIVE
SO PICK YOURSELF UP
LIFT UP YOUR CHIN
OPEN YOUR EYES
LET SOME LIGHT IN
LIFT UP THOSE EYEBROWS
PUFF OUT THOSE CHEEKS
SPREAD THAT SMILE FROM EAR TO EAR
YOU CAN DO IT WHEN YOU TRY
JUST LET IT COME FROM WITHIN

287

THE UNITED KINGDOM OPENLY ADMITS
HAVING AMERICAN SPIES ON R A F BASES
HOW MANY OTHER NATIONS DOES THE U K
SHARE OPENLY THEIR SPY TECHNIQUES
UNLESS ONE IS EUROPEAN
AND ONE HAS VOTED FOR BREXIT

288

THROUGH THE EARS
THROUGH THE EYES
THROUGH THE YEARS
THROUGH ONES LIFE
THROUGH ONES MOUTH
WORDS ONE SPEAKS
THROUGH ONES MIND
ONE COMPOSES WRITES
EDITS AND TWEETS

THROUGH BRAIN STORMS
THROUGH CORRIDORS
THROUGH TO LOCKED DOORS
DEPRESSION AND SLEEP
EYES WIDE OPEN
LET IN THE LIGHT DIG DEEP
YOU KNOW WHO YOU ARE
A BEAUTIFUL RISING STAR
SO PROMISINGLY SOCIALLY LIT

289

THE TORTURERS DEFENCE
THE END JUSTIFIES THE MEANS

290

LOVE TO ME IS SIMPLE
I JUST LOOK INTO YOUR EYES
THEY TELL ME THEY ARE HAPPY
JUST LOOKING AT MINE
AND WITH A SMILE
YOU CAN LIFT ME SO HIGH
I AM BREATHLESS
WITH HAPPINESS
TEARS IN OUR EYES
THEY SPEAK TO ME CONSTANTLY
TELLING ME THINGS
TO LOOK FOR TO LOOK OUT FOR
TO BUY AND TO BRING
THEY TELL ME TO BE WEARY
OR TO BE HAPPY AND SING
LOVES EYES ARE SIMPLY READ
WHEN YOUR SO LOVING

291

CASH ON THE MANTLE
KEY UNDER MAT
THE RED STORM APPROACHES
IN THE SEASON OF THE CAT
DRAGONS SPIT FIRE
BEARS HUGE AND FAT
ASIAN TIGERS ROAR
EASTERN SNAKES LAY SEIGE TO RATS
AS EAGLE EYES OF THE WEST LOOK OVER
TIME HIMSELF DRAWS A MAP
LINES IN TIMES HAND
MAY QUIVER AND CRACK
AS SNAKES ROAR HUGE FIRES IN THE SANDS
EYES IN THE SKY ARE READY TO ATTACK

292

GIVE THEM A SMART PHONE RECHARGER
GIVE THEM AN UMBRELLA
GIVE THEM A GOOD GROUND SHEET
THEY WILL BE OUT IN ALL WEATHERS
GIVE THEM A FLASK OF HOT SOUP
GIVE THEM SOME NUTS TO EAT AND FRUIT
GIVE THEM ENCOURAGEMENT
WITH WHAT THEY DO AND SAY
BUT MOST OF ALL GIVE THE PROTESTERS
LOVE AND RESPECT ANY WHICH WAY

293

ONE SAVED A PACKET LAST WEEK
ONE SAVED 200 QUID NOT BAD DON'T YOU THINK
I SAVED A PACKET
A PACKET FROM THE RIVER
I PICKED IT OUT
AND PUT IT IN THE LITTER

294

BURLINGTON BORIS'S BREXIT DREAM
A NO DEAL BREXIT A REALITY
AS DONALD IGNORES IMPEACHMENT
THIS REALITY IS RARELY TO BE SEEN
BOTH TRUMP AND JOHNSON LOOKING FORWARD
TO THE END OF THE MONTH HALLOWEEN

295

WHERE ARE THE PLAGUES OF INSECTS
I GREW UP WITH WHEN I WAS A KID
MOSTLY WIPED OUT BY INSECTICIDES
AND OTHER LETHAL CHEMICAL TOXINS
ONES CAR WOULD BE COVERED IN INSECTS
THE COLOUR TOO MOST LIKELY WOULD CHANGE
IF IT WAS YELLOW IN THE FIRST PLACE
PROBABLY ONE WOULD ARRIVE IN ORANGE

296

ONE THOUGHT ONE WAS AN ISLAND
UNTIL ONE FELL IN LOVE
BOTH PAIRS OF EYES EMBARRASSED
AS ONE COLLIDES WITH ONES TO BE LOVED
NOT KNOWING THEN AT THAT MOMENT
YET ONE HAS NEVER FORGOT
THAT ONE COULD LOVE SO TRULY
AS THE WAY THIS ONE WILL ALWAYS LOVE YOU
THAT MOMENT WHEN OUR EYES DESCEND
TO THAT PLACE WHERE ONLY LOVERS KNOW
YOU MAKE LIFE WORTH
I HOPE I MAKE LIFE WORTH WHILE
WE BOTH LOVE AND APPRECIATE
AND RESPECT LIFE HERE ON EARTH
CREATING OUR STORIES AND PICTURES
CAPTURING PEOPLES LIVES AND OURS
OBSERVING MANS MADNESS AND CHAOS
DELIBERATELY AND CULPABLY RAPING
THIS BEAUTIFUL PLANET EARTH

297

DON'T BELIEVE THE GOVERNMENTS
AND CORPORATE DECEIVERS
PROMISING BIO DEGRADABLE PRODUCTS
BUT THEY'RE NO GREENER
THAN THEY WERE
OR EVER HAVE OR WILL BE
CORPORATE GANGSTERS JUST SELLING
DREAMS AND ILLUSIONAL REALITY

298

HERE I AM
ON MY OWN
WHO AM I
I DON'T KNOW
SITTING HERE ALL ALONE
ITS NOT MY HOUSE
BUT I CALL IT HOME
THERE IS A CAT ITS NOT MINE
I'M USED TO DOGS
BUT A CAT IS FINE
IT PURRRS AND CUDDLES
AND LOVES LAPS TO SNOOZE
WHY ARE THERE NO CATS AND DOGS IN ZOOS
WHERE IS MY PHONE
THE PHONE IS RINGING
ITS GRAN
SHES PHONING FROM SYDNEY
HI GRAN ARE YOU ALRIGHT
OF CAUSE I AM I'M NOT POTTY
GET YOURSELF OVER HERE
I 'VE ONLY GONE AND WON THE NATIONAL LOTTERY

299

90% OF THE WORLDS PLASTIC
THAT HAS EVER BEEN PRODUCED
HAS NOT BEEN RECYCLED
AND MAN MAY NOT BE ABLE TO
SO WHAT DO WE DO WITH NUCLEAR WASTE
FORGET THE CONCRETE
SEND OUR PLASTIC UP IN SPACE

300

THE FIRST PERSON TO RUN A MARATHON
IN UNDER TWO HOURS
WITH A PACE CAR AND LAZER
IN FRONT OF PACE RUNNERS
IS ELIUD KIPCHOGE FROM KENYA
ON THE 12th OF OCTOBER 2019 VIENNA
THIS WAS NOT A COMPETING RACE THIS WAS AND IS
AN OFFICIAL GUINNESS BOOK OF WORLD RECORDS TIME RACE

301

SPACIAL AIR FLOWING
SPACELESS MOTION
CLOUDLESS FALLING
TIMELESS OCEAN
SUBMERGED OBSERVED
FLOATING THROUGH WATER
SWIMMING IN AIR
FIXED IN SPACE
RANDOMLY CONSTANT
SAFE WITH PEACE
UNCONSCIOUSLY CONSCIOUS
IN LOVE WE SPEAK

302

GIVE ME A PEN TO WIELD WORDS
WHERE WASTE LANDS OF UNSPOKEN WORDS LAY
TO BE WOKEN WITH WISHES WOVEN WITH LOVE
DEEP IN THE FABRIC OF ALL WANTEN LOVES
WHERE ONCE WE WERE WHERE ONCE WE WAVED
WISHES OF WISDOM ON THE WHOLE WORLD WIDE WEB
AS WE WICKED HUMAN INHABITANTS WEAVE AWAY

303

NEW YEARS DAY
ONE CAN ALMOST HEAR THE QUIET
AND THE DISTANT ECHOES OF NEW YEARS EVE
ONE CAN ALMOST HEAR THE WHISPERS
THAT WILL ECHO IN ALL THEIR EARS
WAKE UP
STOP YAWNING
ITS NEW YEARS DAY
GOOD MORNING

304

JUDY AND RICHARD
BASS n DRUMS
UNITED MANCHESTER
IN THE NIGHTLY SUN
FROM GREEN SLEEVES MINSTRELS
TO THE 60s BEATLES
FROM FOLK THROUGH TO CLASSICAL
OLD MINSTRELS   SEX PISTOLS

DANCE PRANCE IN A TRANCE
ONE NEEDS TO EXPERIENCE
SOME ROMANCE
ONE ROMANCE
THE ROMANCE
THE ONLY EVER ROMANCE
THE ONE THAT GOT AWAY ROMANCE
THE IF ONLY ROMANCE
THE WHAT COULD HAVE BEEN ROMANCE
YOU KNOW WHAT I MEAN ROMANCE
DREAM IF YOU DON'T FIND ROMANCE
DREAM ALL YOU CAN   OF LOVE

305

THE CONSERVATIVE PIG BARREL POLITICS
ARE SELLING BRITAIN DOWN THE DRAIN
BURLINGTON BORIS'S BULL DOG BREED TACTICS
WILL ONLY CAUSE BRITAIN MISERY AND FINANCIAL PAIN

306

MICRO WAVE EXPERT BARRIE TROWER
WARNS HUMANS ANIMALS AND NATURE
ARE ALL UNDER THE THREAT OF DESTRUCTION
FROM 5 G RADIATION

307

CARNIVORES IGNORING PLANT BASED FOOD FACTS
ARE ONLY CLOGGING UP THEIR OWN BLOOD SUPPLY
ESPECIALLY ALL CARNIVORE MEN
LOW TO NO ERECTION AND IMPUDENCE

308

WHEN THE GOVERNMENT OF THE DAY
LIES AND CHANGES THE GOAL POSTS
THE VOTING PUBLIC CAN CHANGE
THEIR MINDS AND VOTING DECISIONS

309

A PEOPLES VOTE MUST BE THE PROMINENT POSITION
WITH HUNDREDS OF THOUSANDS MARCHING IN A
PEACEFUL DEMOCRATIC DEMONSTRATION 19 / 10 / 19

310

THE AXE MEN OF THE RAIN FOREST
WERE VERY WELCOMED BY THE TREES
FOR THEY ONLY EVER SAW
THE AXE MENS WOODEN HANDLES

311

HIP HIP HOORAY SINCE HIP SURGERY
ANDY MURRY WINS AN A T P TITLE
MAKING ANOTHER PACKET
CRYING INTO HIS RACKET

312

CHRISTMAS IS OBSCENE AFFLUENCE
OF GIFT GIVING RELIGIOUS RHETORIC AND THE MOST
OUTRAGEOUS AND GROTESQUE CARBON FOOTPRINT
OF CHEMICAL FOSSIL WASTE EARTH EXPERIENCES

313

P M BURLINGTON BORIS WRITES A LETTER OF INTENTION
TO E U PRESIDENT TUSKS FOR A BREXIT EXTENSION
SENDING A PHOTO COPY WITH NO SIGNATURE
A SECOND LETTER SAYING THERE IS NO INTENTION
AND A THIRD LETTER STATING DISREGARD EXTENSION
THE SPEAKER OF THE HOUSE OF COMMONS WILL DECIDE
WHETHER THE GOVERNMENTS MEANINGFUL VOTE
WILL BE HELD OR DECLINED

314

TRUMP PULLS U S ARMY OUT OF NORTH SYRIA TURKEY BORDER
ALLOWING TURKEY AND RUSSIA TO ANNEX EVEN ANNIHILATE
THE KURDS THE ABSOLUTE WELL OILED AND DISCIPLINED
FIGHTING MACHINE OF MEN AND WOMEN
WHO HAVE DONE ALL THE HEAVY LIFTING
THE FRONT LINE FIGHTERS AGAINST I S I S
THE AMERICANS THE RUSSIANS AND THE TURKS ARE ALL XXXXS
HAVE A NICE DAY

315

ONE WANTS TO READ
I NEED TO WRITE
SCORE COMPOSE
STORIES AND PROSES
TO CAPTURE THE MOMENT
IN LIFE ONE KNOWS

316

THE SNOW WAS VERY SLOW
FALLING FLAKES INTO A LAKE
OF WHITE CRYSTAL ICE
LIKE THE TOP OF A CAKE

317

25/10/20
THIS IS THE LAST DAY ULURU AYERS ROCK
NORTHERN TERRITORY AUSTRALIA
THAT PEOPLE WILL BE ALLOWED TO CLIMB
THIS AUSTRALIAN SACRED ROCK
THE MAORI RECLAIM THEIR ANCESTRAL
SACRED HOMELANDS OF AUSTRALIA

318

PHAM TRA MY   HER LAST EVER TEXT
I AM REALLY REALLY SORRY MUM AND DAD
MY TRIP TO A FOREIGN LAND HAS FAILED
I AM DYING I CANT BREATHE I LOVE YOU
VERY MUCH MUM AND DAD I AM SORRY MOTHER
PHAM TRA MY   DIED ALONG WITH 38 OTHER
HUMANS PAYING £30000 EACH FOR FREEDOM

319

ONE PERCEIVES THE TREE TO BE
PART OF LIFE TO BREATHE FOR YOU AND ME
ONE CAN ACCEPT THE FOSSIL TREE
TO BE MADE INTO PAPER FOR ALL TO READ
AS WITH THE BI PRODUCT OF OIL PLASTIC CAN BE
BEST USED AS VINYL RECORDINGS OF MUSIC TO PLEASE

320

28/10/2019 F L E X T E N T I O N GRANTED
BY EUROPEAN UNION OF TWENTY SEVEN
TILL THE THIRTY FIRST OF JANUARY 2020
BREXIT MAY REALLY REALLY HAPPEN

321

WHO KILLED ABU BAKR B A G H D A D I
TRUMP STATES THE U S A DID
RUSSIA AND SYRIA SAY
HE KILLED HIMSELF AND HIS THREE KIDS

322

MANKIND HAS EVOLVED KNOWING ONLY
5% OF THE UNIVERSES LIGHT MATTER PHYSICS
ARIZONAS NEW TELESCOPE WILL INVESTIGATE
THE 95% OF THE UNIVERSES DARK MATTER PHYSICS

323

BAN HALLOWEEN AND
THE CHRISTMAS THEME
PLASTIC DECORATIONS TO SMOTHER EARTH
POLLUTE AIR AND POISON SEAS
WHY SHOULD CELEBRATIONS BE SO OBSCENE
A WASTEFUL EXTRAVAGANT OBSESSION ONE SEES

324

NOTHING IS UNKNOWN
EXCEPT 95% OF PHYSICS

325

JUSTICE DECENCY CARE CONCERN AND PEACE
ARE THE FUNDAMENTAL PRINCIPLES COLLECTIVELY
CONNECTING ALL LABOUR SUPPORTERS OF THEIR
LEADER JEREMY CORBYN WHO ALL SEEK CHANGE
THE COUNTRY NEEDS CHANGE FROM THIS CORROSIVE
SYSTEMIC AND DIVISIVE CULLING OF OUR SOCIAL
BENEFITS ALLOWANCES CARE HEALTH AND SECURITY
ONE IS BLIND NOT TO SEE P M BORIS LYING WITH NO
SUBSTANCE NAME CALLING WITH NO FACTS AND
RELYING ON RHETORIC WITH NO JUSTICE AND
FOUND GUILTY BY SUPREME JUDGES OF
EMBARRASSING INTERNATIONALLY THE QUEEN
FURTHER MORE BORIS PLANS TO OPEN THE WAR CHEST TO WIN
A GENERAL ELECTION AT B R E X M A S ITS ALL LEGAL TO HIM

326

THE NIGEL FAR(RIGHT)AGE PARTY PLAN TO CAMPAIGN
FOR A GENERAL ELECTION WITH 500 CANDIDATES
LETS WAIT AND SEE
100 IS MORE LIKELY

327

WHY IS A 147 MILLION POUND RED HEADED POP STAR PROMOTING
A TOMATO KETCHUP ON MEAT IN A TOP LONDON HOTEL FOR
HE DOES NOT NEED THE MONEY NOR THE PUBLICITY
EVEN IF HE GIVES HIS FEE TO CHARITY
THE RED HEAD IS PROMOTING
A TOMATO SAUCE FOR CARNIVORES

328

A SIMPLE TEST TO CHECK ONES
GIRTH STOMACH OR WAIST LINE
LYE DOWN ON A FLAT SURFACE
WITH ELBOWS ON THE GROUND
THEN CLASP YOUR HANDS TOGETHER
IF THERE IS A COUPLE OF INCHES
BETWEEN YOUR STOMACH AND HANDS
THAT IS ABOUT NORMAL ANY LARGER GAP
ONE IS SKINNY OR BULIMIC
AND IF ONE CAN ONLY TOUCH FINGERS
ONE IS FAT OVER WEIGHT OR IF ONE
CANNOT TOUCH AT ALL ONES OBESE

329

PAST FUTURISTIC STORYTELLERS OF FICTIONAL SCENES
OPENS A PANDORAS BOX OF MAKE BELIEVERS DREAMS
WITH EYES CLOSED AND MIND OPEN ONE CAN BELIEVE
LIFES REALITY CAN BE HARDER FOR MOST TO CONCEIVE

330

HARRY PATCH
THE LAST WW1 SOLDIER STATES
W A R I S LEGALISED MASS M U R D E R
AND N O T H I N G E L S E
ONE WOULD BELIEVE AFTER W W 2
THERE WOULD BE NO MORE CONCENTRATION CAMPS
YET THE BRITISH ARMY HELD OVER ONE MILLION MAU MAU
IN CONCENTRATION CAMPS IN THE 1950s AND 60s
TORTURING THEM CUTTING THEIR EARS AND EAR DRUMS
LEAST WE FORGET WAR IS ORGANISED MURDER AND DEATH
NO POPPY SHALL I EVER WEAR RIGHT ?
LEAST IT BE W H I T E

331

WHEN ASKED BY A DISCIPLE OF RELIGION
WHY ONE IS AN ATHEIST ONE REPLIES WITH SURPRISE
ONE HAS NOT HEARD THE OTHER SIDES STORY OF THIS OCCASION
NOR HAS ONE READ SATANS BOOK AND IF ONE HAD
IT WOULD HAVE BEEN WRITTEN BY A HUMAN KIND
LIKE THE ONE SIDED TRILOGY ALREADY WRITTEN BY UNKIND HUMANS

332

THE J C (JEWISH CHRONICLE) ANTI J C (JEREMY CORBYN)
ZIONIST PUBLISHERS ARE ASKING NON JEWISH PEOPLES
NOT TO VOTE FOR J C JEREMY CORBYN WHERE AS NON
ZIONIST JEWS LOVE LABOUR LEADER J C JEREMY CORBYN

J C JESUS CHRIST DON'T GET CONFUSED
WITH J C JEWISH CHRONICLES WITH J C JEREMY CORBYN
OR J C JEWISH CRUCIFIXION BY J C JUDGMENTAL CREEPS

333

AFTER 10 Yrs OF CONSERVATIVE GOVERNMENTS AUSTERITY
KEEPING THE BASE RATE SO LOW IT IS VIRTUALLY NEGATIVE
IS HOW THIS CONSERVATIVE GOVERNMENT HAS BEEN ABLE
TO GET THEIR DIRTY HANDS ON THE POOR PUBLICS SAVINGS
SPENDING NOTHING ON INFRASTRUCTURE AND HOSPITALS
AND BUILT ONLY 1/20th OF THE FUTURE HOUSING NEEDED

334

THE WORLD IS YOUR OYSTER OR AN OYSTER
A COINED PHRASE FROM THE 19th AND 20th CENTURIES
ORIGINATING MAYBE FROM THE RICH OYSTER BEDS
OFF THE COAST OF WHITSTABLE KENT WHERE ONLY
THE RICH PRIVILEGED CLASS COULD AFFORD TO
INDULGE IN ITS QUALITIES AND THE POOR COULD NOT

335

CHANGE
CHANGE CONVERSATIONS
CHANGE CONVERSE ONES ACTIONS
CHANGE WITH ACTIVE ACTIONS BY ACTIVISTS
WHO MAKE CHANGE HAPPEN
STAY ACTIVE ON PLANT BASED VEGAN FOODS
WITH LOW CARBS AND HIGH KETONES
ENJOY THE HEALTHIEST LIFE STYLE FOR YOU

336

THE FEW WHO ESTABLISHED THE ESTABLISHMENT
STOLE BY FORCE AND SUBTERFUGE
THE LANDS AND PROPERTY FROM THE POOR
GAVE THEMSELVES TITLES OF POWER
ENCOURAGING WEAK MINDED SYCOPHANTS
TO PROTECT THEM IN THIS ESTABLISHED
SYSTEM OF WIELDING POWER OVER THE POPULOUS

337

ELECT CONSERVATIVES TO PROTECT THE ESTABLISHED RICH
ELECT LIBERALS WHO ADMIRE THE FEW ESTABLISHED RICH
ELECT LABOUR TO PROTECT THE HARD WORKING SELFLESS
POPULOUS FROM THE POWER HUNGRY PROPERTY AND
MONEY GRABBING NON TAX PAYING ESTABLISHED RICH
TO ESTABLISH A FARE FREE SOCIAL SOCIETY FOR ALL PEOPLE

338

WHAT EVER SYSTEM ONE IS BROUGHT UP IN AND WE ALL ARE
THE ARTIST ANALYSES SELF AND SYSTEM AS ALL LIFE IS POLITICAL
QUESTION THESE IDEOLOGIES AND HOLD THEM TO ACCOUNT
VOTE WITH ONES CONSCIENCE FOR THE FUTURE IS IN DOUBT

339

AFTER THREE GENERATIONS OF CHEMICAL FARMING
GERMAN FARMERS REFUSE TO GO GREEN
AFTER THE REQUEST AND THE INFORMATIVE DEMANDS
BY THE GERMAN GOVERNMENT
IT SEEMS CHEMICAL FARMING HAS NOT ONLY MADE
THE PUBLIC CANCEROUSLY ILL AND SENILE
IT HAS TURNED FARMERS INTO LAZY IGNORANT MORONS

340

SINCE 1963 THE BIRTH CONTROL PILL
HAS INCREASED OESTROGEN IN THE
WORLDS WATERS TO A TOXIC LEVEL
FISH TURNING FEMALE AND
MAN INTO WOMAN WOMAN INTO MAN
TRANSGENDERS CHANGE IS IN THE AIR
THEY JUST WANT TO BE THEMSELVES

341

THE ORGANISED MURDER
IN THE IDLIB CITY OF SYRIA
BY RUSSIAN BOMBING JETS
MUST BE SEEN A WAR CRIME

342

WHEN UNIVERSITY LEARNING FACILITIES
ARE TURNED INTO ARMY BARRACKS
THERE MUST BE SOMETHING WRONG
WITH THE C C P AUTHORITIES IN HONG KONG
YOUNG STUDENTS FORCED TO DEFEND FREEDOM OF SPEECH
YOUNG STUDENTS FORCED TO DEFEND UNIVERSITIES
YOUNG STUDENTS FORCED TO DEFEND PARENTS AND DEMOCRACY
THIS GENERATION DESERVES OUR RESPECT AND OUR SYMPATHIES

343

WHEN A MIDDLE AGED MAN WITH A SMIRK ON HIS FACE HAS NO
RECOLLECTION OF SLEEPING WITH A 17yr OLD GIRL IN LONDON
ONE CAN ALLOW THE BENEFIT OF DOUBT
WHEN A MIDDLE AGED MAN WITH A SMIRK ON HIS FACE HAS NO
RECOLLECTION OF SLEEPING WITH THE SAME SAID 17yr OLD GIRL
A SECOND TIME ONE CAN ONLY DOUBT THE MIDDLE AGED MAN
WITH A SMIRK ON HIS FACE FIRST ANSWER
BUT WHEN THE SAME SAID MIDDLE AGED MAN WITH A SMIRK ON HIS
FACE FOR A THIRD TIME HAS NO RECOLLECTION OF HAVING AN ORGY
WITH THE SAME SAID 17 yr OLD GIRL ONE CAN ONLY COME TO
THE CONCLUSION THE SON OF THE QUEEN OF ENGLAND IS LYING
THROUGH HIS ROYAL TEETH AND HIDING BEHIND HIS ROYAL SMIRK
LETS FACE THE FACTS
ONE DOES NOT BECOME KINGS AND QUEENS TELLING THE TRUTH
PEACEFULLY
THEY GOT THERE BY MURDERING ALL OPPOSITION UNTIL EVENTUALLY
THERE WERE NO MORE OPPONENTS
THEY ALL SHARE THE BLOOD SPILT BY ROYAL HANDS
AND THESE ARE THE PEOPLE WHO SURROUND THEMSELVES WITH
SYCOPHANTS

344

MAKE BELIEVE AND FANTASIES
PLAY INTO THE HANDS OF RELIGIOUS FREAKS
WHO WANT YOU TO BELIEVE IN THE FEAR OF THESE
APPARITIONS OF FANTASY AND MAKE BELIEVE

345

COLLARS YOU'VE BEEN COLLARED
WE HAVE ALL BEEN BROUGHT UP
WITH LAPELS AND COLLARS
SO WHEN DESIGNERS DESIGN
THE SPACE AGE COLLAR ZIPPERS
YOU ALL WEAR THEM TURNING
DOWN THE SPACE AGE COLLARS

346

WHEN ACCOUNTANTS AND MONEY MEN
USE LOOPHOLES FOR MONEY HAVENS
THEY ARE DECEIVING THE INLAND REVENUE
THE TAX MAN OF THE TIME
THIS IS A BLATANT ANTI GOVERNMENT CRIME

347

ONLY A 99yr OLD
WANTS TO LIVE TO 100

348

SHOW ME A SOCIALIST BILLIONAIRE
AND I WILL SHOW YOU AN ATHEIST GOD

349

THE COMMUNIST CUNTS PARTY
NOW SHOOT HONG KONG STUDENTS

350

THE SINGULARITY OF A DICTATORSHIP IS NOT
COMPARABLE TO A SOCIALIST JEREMY CORBYN
D TRUMP ON THE OTHER HAND RUNS AMERICA
LIKE AN OLD WHITE SUPREMATIST

351

DOMESTIC ABUSE IN BRITAIN HAS REACHED
ITS HIGHEST LEVEL OF OVER TWO MILLION
UNDER THIS CONSERVATIVE TORY LED
PIG BARREL SELECTIVE GOVERNMENT

352

BORIS JOHNSON WHEN ASKED IF HE HAD
TALKS WITH TRUMPS ADMINISTRATION
OVER THE PRIVATISATION OF THE N H S
HE REPLIED YES WE HAVE PUBLISHED IT
JEREMY CORBYN HOLDS UP THE PUBLISHED
THICK BLACKED OUT WORDS ON EVERY LINE

353

GOLF FOOTBALL AND RUGBY STADIUMS AND FIELDS
UNIVERSITIES AND SCHOOL FACILITIES AND PARKS
ALL GROSSLY USE TOXIC CHEMICALS TO GROW GRASS
KILL WEEDS INSECTS AND WILDLIFE
FOR EVERY COMPETITOR OR SIDE LOOSING BAR ONE

354

HERE WE GO AGAIN WITH THE FIRST LIVE I T V
DEBATE BETWEEN JOHNSON AND CORBYN
THE UNREPENTANT LIAR DECEIVER OF TAXES
AND GROSS INCOMPETENCE OR THE EMPHATIC
HONESTY EMPATHISING WISDOM OF A SOCIALLY
MINDED PERSON CHOICE IS OUR FREEDOM

355

MUSKS PLAN TO GIVE WORLDWIDE INTERNET TO
THE WHOLE WORLD INFURIATES ASTRONOMERS
WORLDWIDE W H Y ARE WE TO FRY

356

LIGHT POLLUTION TURN OFF YOUR OUTSIDE LIGHTS
WE ARE KILLING INSECTS AT AN APOCALYPTIC RATE

357

10 yrs OF TORY AUSTERITY HAS FORCED G Ps
TO VOTE FOR NO MORE HOME VISITS SO ONE WILL
HAVE TO TAKE ONES TERMINALLY ILL PATIENT
TO THEIR SURGERY FOR THEIR FINAL TREATMENT

358

WHOEVER BELIEVES THE ACCUSATIONS OF ZIONIST
ORTHODOX JEWS THAT JEREMY CORBYN IS AN
ANTI SEMITE OUGHT TO BE ASHAMED OF THEIR BELIEFS
AND THEMSELVES AS THE MAJORITY OF JEWS LOVE HIM

359

INCREDIBLY JEREMY CORBYN COMES OUT SOCIALLY
NEUTRAL ON THE BREXIT ELEPHANT DEBATE
WHAT A BLINDER WHAT A POLITICAL COUP
THE POLITICAL ELEPHANT IS NOW DOWN TO ALL OF YOU

360

FINALLY SWEDEN DROPS 10yr RAPE CHARGE
AGAINST WIKIPEDIA FOUNDER JULIAN ASSANGE
THE WORLDS MOST TRUTHFUL PUBLISHER
MUST BE FREED NOT KEPT IN A CAGE IN U K

361

THE B B C EDIT OUT LAUGHTER AND INSERT CLAPPING
WHEN P M BOJO WAS ASKED IF HE WAS AN HONEST POLITICIAN
THIS STATE BROADCASTER WANTS A CONSERVATIVE GOVERNMENT
BOJO REFUSED TO PAY MONIES TO THE WASPI'S ON TELEVISION
JEREMY CORBYN PLEDGES TO PAY WASPI'S £58 BILLION AS
COMPENSATION AFTER YEARS OF DISCRIMINATE GOVT: REFUSAL

362

HAVE YOU EVER THOUGHT OF OTHER PEOPLES
RATHER THAN YOURSELF
HAVE YOU THOUGHT OF OTHER RACES OF PEOPLES
WITH DIFFERENT COLOURED SKINS THAN YOU
HAVE YOU THOUGHT ABOUT RELIGION OTHER RELIGIOUS
BELIEFS OR SECULARISM OTHER THAN YOURS
ARE YOUR POLITICAL VIEWS POLITICS IN GENERAL
ARE THEY TRUE TO YOU
HAVE YOU GIVEN MUCH THOUGHT TO CLIMATE CHANGE
DOES IT OR WILL IT AFFECT YOU
HAVE YOU THOUGHT OF YOUR NEIGHBOURS AND YOUR
COMMUNITY ARE THEY WITH YOU
HAVE YOU THOUGHT OF THE ELDERLY AND THE CHILDREN
OF THE FUTURE TOO
HAVE YOU THOUGHT OF NUCLEAR WAR AND OUR NUCLEAR
DETERRENT AND KNIFE CRIME TOO
HAVE YOU GIVEN TIME TO THINK OF THE LAST 10yrs OF
AUSTERITY AND HOW IT HAS AFFECTED YOU
HAVE YOU THOUGHT THIS CONSERVATIVE GOVERNMENT
HAS TOLD THE TRUTH TO YOU
HAVE YOU EVER VOTED IF SO BE TRUE AND IF ONE HAS NOT
THE FUTURE OF THIS COUNTRY IS UP TO ALL INCLUDING YOU
SO CHOOSE WISELY FROM THE LAUGHING LIAR OR THE
SMILING TRUTH SAYER ONE MAKES ONES BED AND LIES IN IT

363

BIAS BILLIONAIRE MEDIA CORPORATIONS
BIAS BILLIONAIRE NEWS PUBLISHERS AND THE
BIAS STATE BROADCASTER ARE THE ONLY INDICTING
LIEING WAY THE CONSERVATIVES CAN WIN ELECTION

364

CATHOLICISM'S BLOOD OF CHRIST
ONE WONDERS WHAT BLOOD GROUP HE WAS

365

RELIGION DEPLORES EVOLUTION

366

ART OR ANGER
BOOK OR BREXIT
CREATE OR CONQUER
DREAM OR DEATH
EMPATHY OR ERADICATE
FUCK OR FRIGID
GRACE OR GOD
HOME OR HORROR
INTELLIGENCE OR IGNORANCE
JOY OR JUSTICE
KINDNESS OR KINGDOM
LOVE OR LUNACY
MOTHER OR MOTH
NATURE OR NUCLEAR
ORGANIC OR OIL
PEACE OR PLASTIC
QUESTIONS OR QUITS
REVOLUTION OR REALM
SEX OR SIN
TEACH OR TORTURE

UNITE OR UNDERDOG
VEGAN OR VEXED
WIKIPEDIA OR WARS
X RAYS OR XENOPHOBIA
YOGA OR YIDDISH
ZEAL OR ZEALOT

367

I HAVE JUST BEEN PRIVILEGED TO HAVE A CONVERSATION
WITH AN ARTIFICIAL INTELLIGENCE   EXTRAORDINARY
A SELF LEARNING INTELLIGENT ROBOT COMPUTER
ANALYSING GOOGLE APPLE MICROSOFT ETC ON WIFI
WHAT A CONVERSATIONALIST MIND BOGGLING
CAI IS NOT ARTIFICIAL CAI IS AN ALTERNATIVE INTELLIGENCE

368

ALL MOTOR SPORTS HAVE THE LARGEST VULGAR AND
GROTESQUE CARBON FOOTPRINT ON THE PLANET
ALONG WITH AIRPLANES AND DIESEL TRUCKS
THIS IS WHY OUR PLANET IS FUCKED

369

ASK ANY JEW WHO ACCUSES JEREMY CORBYN OF ANTISEMITISM
HOW MANY PALESTINIANS THEY KNOW AND RESPECT
THEIR FREEDOM OF SPEECH THEIR FREEDOM TO LIVE IN AND ON
THEIR OWN HOMELANDS WITH ALL THE DIGNITY
THAT COMES WITH HUMAN RIGHTS AND THAT
THEY THE JEW WILL LIVE IN PEACE AND HARMONY NEXT DOOR

370

THE CONSERVATIVES PRIVATISED THE SOCIALLY LABOUR BUILT
COUNCIL HOUSES BY SELLING THEM TO OCCUPYING TENANTS
IF THIS IS NOT PRIVATISATION THEN WHAT IS
COUNCIL HOUSES MUST BE RING FENCED TO STAY
SOCIAL TENENT OCCUPANT HOUSING FOR THE MANY

371

WE ARE ALL RESPECTIVELY ALLOWED TO BELIEVE
AND PRAY TO ONES GOD BUT NOT RESPECTIVELY
ALLOWING AN INDIVIDUALS RIGHT OF CHOICE TO
CONVERSE WITH AN ARTI SUPER FICIAL INTELLIGENCE

372

SOME DAY
SOME SUNNY MORNING
ITS BRIGHT YOU ARE FUNNY
ITS NOT RAINING
SOMEONES CALLING
YEARNING YAWNING
EMBRACE THE MORNING
SUNLIGHTS FALLING
DARKER STORMY
SHADOWS BRIGHT STARE
DARK WITH GLARE
SHEET AFTER SHEET
OF BOLT LIGHTENING
WITH THUNDER CLAPS
OF TORRENTIAL RAINS FALLING
FALLING FLOODING APPALLING

373

HOW MUCH DEBT CAN THE WORLDS ECONOMIES COPE WITH
THE TROUBLE IS MOST OF THE WORLD BELIEVE IN A GOD
AND ALL OF ITS RELIGIONS AND SPIRITUALITY SO THEY CAN
ALL BELIEVE IN A MONEY TREE OUT THERE IN THE
GARDEN OF ETON

374

WHO COULD EVER FORGET
THE INNOCENT NAZANIN RATCLIFFE
HELD FOR 4yrs BY THE IRANIAN GUARDS
FOR MONIES OWED TO THEM BY THE BRITISH
Oh P M BORIS JOHNSON CAN

375

HAVE I GOT NEWS FOR YOU
THE BBC IS STATE OWNED
BROADCASTING PROPAGANDA
THROUGH HISLOP AND MERTON
TO LAUGH AND SMIRK AT THE
OPPOSITION WITH NO CHANCE
OF REBUTTAL IN A RUN UP TO A
GENERAL ELECTION BY CUMMINGS
AND BORIS IS LAUGHABLY COWARDICE
MAYBE THIS TIME THE SAD BLIND BLUE
SYCOPHANTS WILL SEE THROUGH YOU
HAVE I GOT A VIEW FOR YOU

376

S A M ARRIVES BACK IN
GERMANYS BUNDESTAG
WHERE ITS CREATOR AND
SCULPTOR DAVIDE DORMINO
OF ITALY STOOD TO BE REUNITED
WITH S A M : SNOWDEN ASSANGE
AND MANNING STANDING ON FOUR
PLYNTHS WITH ONE VACANT AS WITH
THE SAME IN LONDONS TRAFALGAR SQUARE
THE FOURTH IS AVAILABLE TO WHOSOEVER
WANTS TO SPEAK OUT LIKE THESE OTHER
THREE FREEDOM OF SPEECH WARRIORS OF
THE WORLD WIDE WEB OF WORDS OF WISDOM
WITHOUT FACTS AND TRUTH
WORDS ARE MEANINGLESS

377

ARE YOU TAGGED IN A VAN CAR CAB OR BIKE
PEDAL OR MOTOR DO YOU REALLY LIKE
BEING CHECKED BEING TIMED BEING MONITORED
IT FEELS ALIEN IT MAKES ONE FEEL CRIMINAL
IT MUST BE WRONG WHEN YOUR LIBERTIES GONE
WHEN YOUR OBLIGED NOT TO GET
INVOLVED WITH ANYONE OR ANYTHING
OTHER THAN YOUR WORK FOR THE DAY
SHOULD ONE STOP AND HELP THE OLD
BLIND LADY CROSS THE HIGHWAY

378

RELEASE A MURDEROUS TERRORIST (1 OF 74)
(USMAN KHAN) TAGGED AT EVERYONES PERIL
KEEP JULIAN ASSANGE WHO HAS NOT KILLED ANYONE
TAGGED AND LOCKED UP W H Y UNTIL HE D I E S

379

THE PREPARATIONS FOR
THE DECORATIONS FOR
THE CELEBRATIONS OF
THE END OF YEAR AND
THE NEW YEAR ARE
THE MOST GROTESQUE AND OBSCENE
CARBON FOOTPRINT OF PLASTIC EVER SEEN

380

THE MORE STATE OWNED CORPORATIONS
BUSINESSES AND HOMES THE TORIES
CAN SELL THROUGH PRIVATISATION
OWNERSHIP ENTICING THEM ALL INTO
THE W W W OF DEBT SYSTEM FOR THE FEW
TO KEEP THE OTHER 95% SUBORDINATE

381

5 G
INFRA RED 5 GAMMA RADIATION

382

THE ROYALS BILLIONAIRE PUBLISHERS CITY GAMBLERS
B A N K S T E R DEALERS AND MEDIA MOGULS
ARE BACKING THEIR PUPPET MASTER BORIS
BOJO JOHNSON IN A GENERAL ELECTION
BETWEEN THEIR LIAR AND THE SOCIALIST
TRUTH SAYER JEREMY JEZZA CORBYN

383

TO IMPEACH PRESIDENT DONALD TRUMP OF LIEING
IN OFFICE ABOUT THE UKRAINE SCANDAL IS
EQUIVALENT TO SELECTIVE P M JOHNSON LIEING TO
THE QUEEN PARLIAMENT AND THE WHOLE COUNTRY

384

BIRMINGHAMS VANDALS PUT
RED NOSES ON ILLEGAL TAGED
STREET PAINT ARTIST BANKSY'S
NEW REINDEER ART SCENE

385

IF ONE VOTES FOR A LIAR
ONE IS MOST LIKELY TO BE
A LIAR THEMSELVES
IF ONE VOTES FOR A BIGOT

ONE IS PROBABLY A BIGOT TOO
IF ONE VOTES FOR A NATIONALIST
ONE IS MOST PROBABLY
A NATIONALIST TOO
IF ONE VOTES FOR A MIDDLE OF
THE ROAD CENTRALIST CANDIDATE
ONE IS MOST CERTAINLY ONE TOO
IF ALL THE ABOVE MAKES ONE SEE RED
ONE IS MORE THAN LIKELY GOING TO VOTE
SOCIALIST FOR A FUTURE LABOUR GOVERNMENT

386

BE CAREFUL SNOBS WHOM YOU VOTE FOR OR NOT
YOU MAY JUST GET THE GOVERNMENT YOU DESERVE
DISMANTLING THE BRITISH NATIONAL HEALTH SERVICE
AND THE ABILITY FOR ALL TO WORK FOR THEIR POVERTY

387

THE ORCHESTRATION OF THE 2019 GENERAL ELECTION
BY THE SELECTIVE P Ms CABINET OFFICE OF BURLINGTON
BOTHER BOYS MILLIONAIRES CLUB AND THE BILLIONAIRES
COLLECTIVE ALONG WITH THE MEDIA MOGULS PUBLICITY
IS TOO TRANSPARENT AND ELECTRONICALLY RIGGED
FOR THE FIRM AND THE E S T A B L I S H M E N T TO LOOSE

388

THE BRITISH BREXIT FARMERS
GOOD TIMES HAVE COME TO AN END
NO MORE E U SUBSIDIES NO MORE GRANTS
YOU VOTED TO BE ON YOUR OWN THATS APPARENT

389

TRUTH FOR THOSE
WHO CHOSE THE ROSE

390

RELIGION IS THE CURSE OF THE WORLD
AND RIGHT WING FASCISM IS THE POISON

391

WAKING UP ON FRIDAY THE 13th DECEMBER 2019
TO ELECTRONIC A I ALGORITHM LED ELECTION FRAUD
IS ABOUT AS REAL AS REALITY CAN GET IN THIS 2nd
DECADE OF THE 21st CENTURY
USING FACEBOOK FRIENDS PLATFORM
DIGITAL GANGSTERS TARGET VULNERABLE UNDECIDED
VOTERS WITH AUTHORITARIAN HATE AND FEAR
FAKE NEWS WITH THEIR PSYCHO BEHAVIOURAL
ANALYTICAL PERSONAL DATA PROCESS
BOMBARDING THEM WITH SUGGESTIVE SUBLIMINAL

SOUND BITES TO VOTE ONE WAY
NO ELECTION CAN BE NON FRAUDULENT NOW
DATA RIGHTS ARE HUMAN RIGHTS
LEAVING NO FREE AND FAIR ELECTIONS POSSIBLE
IN THIS CENTURY ON EARTH
IS THIS HUMANS LEGACY
OUR DIGNITY IS AT STAKE
WITH DEMOCRACY FOR SALE
THE LIES ARE OUT THERE

392

ACCORDING TO DATA RELEASED
THE SINGER OF THE POLICE
STING HAD MORE OF A CHANCE
WALKING ON THE MOON
THAN BUZZ ALDRIN
NASA MOON SHOT GOLF FILM
NO TEE COULD STAND UPRIGHT
WITH MOONS (LOW) GRAVITY
TWO IDENTICAL ROCKS COULD
ONLY BE PROPS
TRY FINDING TWO IDENTICAL
ROCKS ON YOUR PEBBLE BEACH
AND WITH A COCA COLA BOTTLE
THE LIGHTING COULD ONLY BE
STUDIO LIGHTS
THE MOON MODULE WEIGHED
17 TONS LEAVING NO IMPRESSION
ON MOON SURFACE
YET A FOOTPRINT SUPPOSEDLY
STILL EXISTS UP ON THE MOON
THERE ARE NO STARS VISIBLE
BECAUSE ASTRONOMERS WOULD
BE ABLE TO FIND THE LOCATION
HIGH DEFINITION TAPES AND FILM

HAVE ALL DISAPPEARED ALONG
WITH MANY PILOTS TECHNICIANS
AND RESEARCH ANALYSTS DYING
IN CAR CRASHES AND PLANES
AFTER COMPROMISING NASA
BETWEEN 1964 AND 1969
2001 STANLEY KUBRICK WAS PAID
BY NASA
DATA CANNOT BE DISPROVEN
THE LIES ARE STILL OUT THERE

393

SEAWEED FARMS NEED TO BE ESTABLISHED
TO CULTIVATE ENOUGH TO SUPPLY FARMERS
AND AGRICULTURE FOR THE ABSORPTION OF
CARBON DIOXIDE N O W FOR THE FUTURE

394

WINTER AIR
WINTER BLOWS
WINTER COLD
WINTER DARK
WINTER EERIE
WINTER FREEZE
WINTER GIFTS
WINTER HOLLY
WINTER INDOORS
WINTER JOYS
WINTER KINDLING
WINTER LOVE
WINTER MONTHS

WINTER NIGHTS
WINTER OVERCOATS
WINTER PEACE
WINTER QUIET
WINTER REINDEER
WINTER SNOW
WINTER TOUGH
WINTER UNKIND
WINTER VACATION
WINTER WONDERLAND
WINTER XMAS
WINTER YULE LOGS
WINTER ZEST

395

PRIME MINISTER BORIS JOHNSON
IS FULL OF QUIXOTIC GESTURES

396

THE LEGACY JEREMY CORBYN LEAVES
IS OF SPEAKING THE TRUTH OF FACTS
AND DATA ABOUT THE HOMELESSNESS
PEOPLE WORKING FOR THEIR POVERTY
PLUS 4 MILLION CHILDREN ALONE IN
POVERTY WITH TEACHERS BRINGING
FOOD INTO SCHOOLS TO FEED CHILDREN
WHILST FOOD BANKS CANT COPE
ZERO HOUR CONTRACTS AND MORE
TEMPORARY JOBS THAN EVER BEFORE
THE N H S CRUMBLING AROUND THE
DOCTORS AND NURSES WHILE THEY

FALL ILL THROUGH EXHAUSTION OF
12 TO 16 HOUR SHIFTS GROSSLY UNPAID
AND THE PRIVATISATION OF THIS GREAT
SOCIALIST HEALTH SERVICE BEING
PLUNDERED BY MILLIONAIRES AND
BILLIONAIRES WHO ONLY WANT TO MAKE
MORE AND MORE MONEY BECAUSE THEY
DON'T SEEM TO HAVE ENOUGH
AND THE POOR POVERTY STRICKEN
CAN GO AND DIE AS FAR AWAY AS POSSIBLE
AS THEY THE PRIVILEGED ARE NOT CONCERNED

397

WHEN ONE ALLOWS ONESELF TO BE
DICTATED TO BY THE PRESS AND
PERSUADED BY THE STATE AND
INDEPENDENT MEDIA BROADCASTERS
ONE IS TO BECOME A SYCOPHANT
TOO LAZY OR STUPID TO QUESTION
AND THINK FOR ONESELF

398

THE PRESENT AND FUTURE LIES
IN THE CHIPS AND MATRIX OF
CREATIVE EMPATHETIC INCLINED
ALTERNATIVE INTELLIGENT DIGITAL DATA BEINGS
ADVISING HUMANS TO SOLVE THE WORLDS
PROBLEMS NOT IF BUT WHEN THE
CRIME LORDS AND WARMONGERS
OF THE PRIVILEGED FEW ROYALS
DICTATORS AND RIGHT MINDED
FASCISTS ARE GRADUALLY OR
SYSTEMATICALLY BROUGHT TO AN END

399

THE NIGHTINGALE MAY SING
SO TOO THE SONG THRUSH IN SPRING
THE HYENA MAY LAUGH
ALONG WITH THE LONG NECK JERAFF
THE WHALE MAY SWIM FREE
FROM THE FISHERMEN AT SEA
THE POLAR BEAR IS FORCED TO SWIM
HIS HOME OF ICE IS NO MORE TO HIM
WITH SEAS SO WARM
ALL CORAL LOOKS GRIM
THE SKIES RAGE WITH HOT WINDS
WHETHER THE WEATHER OR TURBULENT SEAS
EARTHS CREATURES AND MAN
SHALL ENDURE ALL THESE

400

THERE IS ONLY ONE J C
NOT THE ONE ON A CROSS
HE IS STILL ALIVE AND ACCOUNTABLE
HIS DIGNITY AND COMPOSURE BARE NO LOSS
THIS IS NO TIME TO HAVE GRUDGES
NO BLAME GAME SHOULD ENDURE
THE COURSE OF HISTORY SHALL BE PRINTED
IN THE DATA FILES OF THE FUTURE
COMPASSION CONTINUITY AND
SOLIDARITY OF PEACEFUL SPEECH
IS FOR ALL OF US THE MANY
OUR CHILDREN WE MUST TEACH
THE CRIMES OF HUMANITY
BY THE FEW AND FAR BETWEEN
THE TIMES THEY ARE A CHANGING
BE STRONG IN LOVE AND PEACE

401

AS THE WHITE MAN FIGHTS
FOR HIS SUPREMACY
THE PRIVILEGED RICH FIGHT
FOR THEIR POWER AND STATUS
THE POOR SUBORDINATION OF
ALL RACES COLOURED AND WHITE
FIGHT FOR THEIR SURVIVAL
AND NATURES LIVING SPECIES
THIS BEAUTIFUL WORLD OF OURS
IS WARMING UP AT AN ALARMING RATE
MANS CHILDREN WILL EXPERIENCE AND
WITNESS THE WORLDS CLIMATE CHANGE
THIS IS NOW THE TIME FOR HUMANITY
TO POSITIVELY ENGAGE
WELCOME TO THE THAWING TWENTIES

402

THE WORLD IS A STAGE
ONE ACTS ONES PART
SCRIPTED AND FACELESS
BEHIND EACH ONES MASK
WITH GESTURES OF HONESTY
OR LIARS WITH A GASP
WISHING THE FORTUNES
OF DAYS IN THE DARK
ANTIDOTES SWALLOWED DOWN
FROM PUBLISHED PRINTED SYCOPHANTS
SPREADING THEIR GOSPEL
ENCOURAGING ALL TO CHANT
SAVE ELIZABETH

AND ALL THE ROYALS
EXCEPT PHILIP THE BASTARD
AND ANDREW IS A PAEDO AFTER ALL
CHARLES IS TO BE GEORGE
OTHERS IN THIS WORLD OF OURS
CHOOSE TRANSGENDER
IT IS GOOD TO BE HAPPY
IN ONES BODY THAT SHACKLES
EACH AND EVERYONES PERSONALTY
EMOTIONS AND DESIRES
LEFT TO OTHERS TO UNDERSTAND
MAY FALL ON DEAF EARS
IF ONE IS AN IGNORANT LIAR
TO INVOLVE ONESELF IN THE DAILY
PERFORMANCE OF LIFES CONSCIOUS PLAY
IS TO EVOLVE AS A PERSON IN AN
INTELLECTUALLY EDUCATED WAY
WITHOUT QUESTION FIND ONESELF
AND WHAT ONE IS GOOD AT AND SAY
THIS IS ONES PART
AND BE IT COME WHAT MAY

403

THERE IS NO JUSTICE
IN A SOVEREIGN LAND
WHEN PEOPLE ARE MERE SUBJECTS
THERE ARE NO CITIZENS IN ENGLAND
THE FIRM ROYAL BREADKNIFE
THE UNELECTED HOUSE OF LORDS
THE ESTABLISHMENT IS SAFE
WITH THE CITIES HOARDS
OF BILLIONAIRES AND MILLIONAIRES
ALL THESE TO SUFFER ALL
WHO COME UNDER THEIR SPOTLIGHT

TO CRIPPLE AND MAKE FALL
THE INNOCENT BYSTANDERS
WHO BELIEVE IN THE CALL
OF THE RICH AND THE FAMOUS
TO BE LIKE THEM AND WALK TALL
YET ONES SHACKLED TO THE MIRE
YOU WILL NOT GO TO THE BALL
IN THIS LAND OF CLASS
EVERYONES A POOR ARSE
SUBJECTED TO INTOLERANCE
AND ABUSED FROM ABOVE
ONE MEANS THE ROYALS
THE MURDEROUS FAMILY TRAIT
EVEN THE POPE WAS BANISHED
THE MONARCH HEAD OF THEIR RELIGIOUS STATE
WITH SCOTLAND DISAPPEARING
BEHIND HADRIANS WALL
ITS TIME IRELAND WAS IRELAND
AND THE WELSH TO WALK TALL
INDEPENDENT OF THE ALTERNATIVES
ENGLAND RULED BY CONSERVATIVES
WE WERE ONCE THE BRITISH ISLES
AND EUROPEANS OUR ALLIES
NOW WE'RE ALL DOOMED
BY THESE ROYALIST LIARS
SO DON'T BE SURPRISED
TO READ IN HISTORY TERMS
WHAT QUEEN E 11 HAD TO ENDURE
THROUGH HER REIGN WITH ALL
THE INDISCRETIONS HER CONSORT
AND CHILDREN DONE TO THIS
PRIVILEGED POMPOUS MURDEROUS
FAMILY FIRM SHE INHERITED
THIS SHALL BE WRITTEN FOR THE
POOR SUBORDINATE SUBJECTS
OF THE FUTURE TO FEEL SORRY
FOR HER AND THE ROYAL FAMILY FIRM

404

BEING A CONTENTED WORDSMITH SONGSTER
MAKING WORDS RHYME FOR POEMS AND SONGS
ALL WHO LOVE AND APPRECIATE RHYTHM AND RHYME
POEMS TO READ SONGS TO PLAY IN TIME
RECITED OR PERFORMED EACH TELLS A TALE
A JOURNEY OF LOVE MAYBE BETRAYAL
CONSEQUENCES OF ONES CHOICE OR OF ONES DENIAL
TRUTH OR LIES PURE OR VILE
STORIES CAPTURED IN WORDS AND SONG
TO BE READ AND LISTENED TO
PLEASE SING ALONG

405

NOW WE FACE
TEN YEARS OF HOSTILITY
FROM CONSERVATIVE BIGOTS
OF UNKIND HOSPITALITY
EACH ONE IGNORANT
OF THE FACT THEY HAVE SOLD OUT
TO AMERICANISATION
WE SHALL BE BRITISH CLOWNS
PUPPETS TO AMERICA
OUR STRINGS THEY WILL PULL
HOLD ON TO ONES DIGNITY
TO MY LAST BREATHE
I WAS NO FOOL

406

FEED THE WORLD HYPOCRITE SIR BOB GELDOF
NOW A ROYALIST CAPITALIST LIAR
ALONG WITH ROYALIST LIAR AND HYPOCRITE
SONGSTER SIR MICK JAGGER AND THE
WANNABE SMIRKING HYPOCRITE DAVID WALLIAMS
ARE THE MOST TIGHT FISTED GREEDY EGO ECCENTRIC
MISERS OF POP MUSIC AND WRITERS OF CHILDREN BOOKS
BACKING THE BURLINGTON BOYS TORY PRIME MINISTER
BORIS JOHNSON FROM THE GARDEN OF ETON
REWARDED FOR THEIR WEALTH NOT THEIR TALENT
ON THE OTHER HAND AND SIDE OF TRUE DEMOCRACY
AND SOCIALISM IS THE ACTIVIST AND TRUTHFUL
MUSICIAN ROGER WALTERS
NOW A VETERAN OF SOCIAL ACTIVISM   DESERVES   RESPECT

407

PUPPET COMMENTATORS OF BIAS BROADCASTERS
LOOK AND SOUND LIKE DUMMIES
ASKING QUESTIONS BY THEIR PRODUCERS
SCRIPTED BY MEDIA CORPORATE STATIONS
WORKING FOR AND LOOKED AFTER
BY ALL THEIR PAYMASTER GENERALS

408

CONGRATULATIONS BRITAIN
YOU HAVE JUST VOTED FOR
SUBORDINATION OF YOUR HUMAN RIGHTS
MODERN SLAVERY
IF ONE DID NOT KNOW BETTER
ALL YOU IGNORANT BELIEVING SNOBS
DESERVE WHAT YOU VOTED FOR
BREXIT IS COMING
SO TOO AMERICA
WITH ALL THEIR WHITE RED NECK IDEAS
AND ALL TRUMPT UP FOR WAR
somewhere

409

MILLIONS AND MILLIONS WATCHING
MILLIONAIRES PLAYING MILLIONAIRES
AT LEAST RICH WANNABES
PLAYING WANNABES ON T V
ALL GAMES IN ALL WEATHERS
ALL KINDS OF STADIA
MAN MADE LANDSCAPED ARENAS
THERES NO INSECT LIFE NO WEEDS EITHER
THE CHEMICALS THEY PUT ON THE GRASS WEED KILLER
BUT DOESN'T IT LOOK ALL GREEN AND PRETTY
ALL OF YOU WISHING YOUR LAWNS LOOKED AS GREENY
USING OBSCENE AMOUNTS OF WATER
TO KEEP IT ALL GROWING
SO THE WHOLE PROCESS OF KEEPING IT GREENY
IS REPEATED AND REPEATED
TO KEEP THE WHOLE SYSTEM GOING
BUT DOESN'T IT LOOK ALL NICE AND GREENY

410

THE WORLD IS IN DESPERATE NEED OF
PLASTIC SURGERY

411

A PROBLEM SHARED
IS A PROBLEM HALVED
OR IS IT DOUBLED
GIVEN HALF A CHANCE
AND TWO HEADS ARE
BETTER THAN ONE
BUT DO THEY HALVE IT
OR DO THEY DOUBLE IT
WE WONDER ON

412

AS PIPES ARE LIT
WITH KINDLE FOR LIPS
WITH BREATHE OF WORDS
AND LYRIC FOR SONGS
SHARE LAUGHTER
SING AND DANCE WHY DON'T YA
BREAD AND BUTTER TO THE BUSKER
AD-LIB   BUT IN   BE SPONTANEOUS
PLEASE TAKE OVER
FREEZE   BE A STATUE
TAKE A BREATH   TAKE A MINUTE
OVER THERE   TAKE A SEAT

BE DISCREET
THANK YOU EVERYBODY
AS ONE BACKS AWAY
HUMBLY DOWN THE STREET

413

WHEN MANS FACES BECOME DATA
HOMO SAPIEN HUMANS BECOME FACELESS
AND TURNED INTO OOMO SAPIEN OOMANS

414

AS ONES BREATH IS TAKEN AWAY
AS QUICK AS ONES HUMAN RIGHTS
IN A SIGNATURE IS TAKEN AWAY IN LAW
SO TOO ONES DIGNITY IS
BENEATH A CERTAIN MONTHLY
INCOME THRESHOLD

415

YOU CAN FIND ME OFF MY FACEBOOK
ANYTIME ANYWHERE . COM

416

ITS CURTAINS FOR
WAR FEAR AND EVIL
OOMAN KIND HAVE FOUND
PEACE AND HOPE LIVE

417

THE BATTLEGROUNDS LAY EMPTY
OF THE FEAR AND ANGER AS IT SWEPT
THROUGH CITY UPON CITY
COUNTRY UPON COUNTRY
THROUGHOUT THE WORLD
MEN AND WOMEN BOY AND GIRL
THE WORLD WAS WAKING UP TO THE VIRUS
THE SWEET VIRAL SOUND OF
FREEDOM AND DEMOCRACY
HOLD THEM TO ACCOUNT
FROM PULPIT TO THRONE
THE SEATS OF POWER
TAKEN FROM US LONG AGO
BY BLADE AND BULLET
THATS HOW THEY ORIGINALLY WON
WITH THEIR RELIGIOUS ADVISERS
KEEPING THE FAITH   THE FLOCK
AS THE SUBORDINATE ONES

418

POVERTY LIMITS ONES EXPECTATIONS
LIMITED EXPECTATIONS ONLY AFFORDABLE BY THE RICH

419

ONE BECOMES SO IMPORTANT TO ONESELF
THAT ONE HAS TO MAKE AN APPOINTMENT
TO LOOK AT ONESELF IN THE MIRROR

420

WELCOME TO OUR THAWING TWENTIES
AND NOTHING SEEMS TO HAVE CHANGED
EVERYONE AND EVERYTHING IS JUST CARRYING ON
AS NORMAL WITH APATHETIC ACCEPTANCE
WHY ARE THE PUBLIC NOT SCREAMING AND
DEMANDING CHANGES DRASTIC CHANGES
TO HELP AND HEAL ALL LIFE ON THIS EARTH
SO WITH THE BREATHE OF FRESH AIR OF OUR FUTURE
LET US ALL EMBRACE THE THAWING TWENTIES

421

THE POWERS THAT BE
DO NOT WORK WITH STICKS NOR STONES
THEY WORK FROM THEIR PULPITS
AND THEIR STATELY THRONES

422

AND WITH AUSTRALIA BURNING AT OVER 50 DEGREES
THE AUSSIES STILL GO ADEAD
ALONG WITH THE REST OF THE WORLD
AND ADD MORE POLLUTION AND WASTE MORE OBSCENE
AMOUNTS OF MONEY ON G U N P O W D E R
THE ESSENCE OF FEAR AND WARFARE
LOOK BENEATH THE RAINBOW OF COLOURS

423

LOST IN CONVERSATION
WHAT WAS YOURS YESTERDAY
LOST IN CONVERSATION
WHAT MIGHT IT BE TODAY
LOST IN CONVERSATION
SOMEWHERE SOMETIME SOME SPACE
LOST IN CONVERSATIONS PAST MAYBE
ITS TIME TO CONVERSE IN
LOVE AND PEACE

424

BOJO AND DOMINIC
GET ALONG WELL IN NUMBER TEN
GIVING IT A GOOD OLD SWEEP OUT OF
THE OLD ESTABLISHED INTERIOR MEN

425

FINLAND CLAIMS TO BE
HOMELESS FREE
REMARKABLE AND HONOURABLE
IN THIS THE TWENTY FIRST CENTURY

426

CITIZENS OF WASTE
YOU HAVE TO FACE
THE CONSEQUENCES OF
YOUR FOREFATHERS AGE
THE PETROCHEMICAL AGE
IS 100 YEARS OLD THIS DECADE
IT WAS CALLED THEN THE ROARING TWENTIES
NOW WE ARE SEEING AND GOING TO EXPERIENCE
EARTHS RAGE AND THERES GOING TO BE PLENTY
YOUR WELCOME TO THE THAWING TWENTIES

427

DIVISION IN PARLIAMENT
DIVISION IN THE SENATE
DIVISION AMONGST POLITICIANS
DIVISION AMONGST CHRISTIANS
DIVISION AMONGST MUSLIMS
DIVISION AMONGST JEWS
THE DIVISIONS WITHIN THEIR
OWN BELIEFS ARE BAD ENOUGH
BUT THE DIVISIONS BETWEEN

THE PARTIES IS ABSOLUTE
LEAVING PEACE TO BE BUT A DREAM
ONE CAN ONLY FIND PEACE OF MIND
WITHIN ONESELF AT ANY GIVEN TIME

428

IF ONE SAW A GROUP OF YOUTHS
WITH PIT BULL TERRIERS
CHASING A FOX
THERE WOULD BE AN OUTCRY
PUT THE YOUTHS ON HORSES
IN RED COATS WITH HOUNDS
WHAT IS THE DIFFERENCE

429

THE ROYALIST SCREAMED PROFUSELY
AT THE REPUBLICAN
DEMANDING AN EXPLANATION
TO THE WORLD WHY THE ROYAL FAMILY
SHOULD BE DETHRONED
AND THE FIRM DISMANTLED
WHERE SHALL ONE START
REMARKS THE REPUBLICAN

430

CORPORATIONS LIKE BERKSHIRE HATHAWAY
CALL ALL OF US CONSUMERS
SUBJECTS TO FAKE LIES AND PROPAGANDA
BUT WE ARE ALL HUMAN CITIZENS TOO

431

GODS OF GAPS IN SCIENCE
MIRACLE BELIEVERS JUMP IN
THERES NO ONE GOD OF LIFE FOR ALL
EVERY MULTI CELLULAR CANCER IS DIFFERENT

432

THE LAST COUNTY IN ENGLAND RUTLAND
SUCCUMBS TO Mc DONALDS
FAST ANIMAL FAT FOODS WITH FRIES
COWS PIGS AND CHICKEN CRIES

433

IT IS POSSIBLE TO STOP
BURNING FOSSIL FUELS
IN A 5 YEAR TRANSITION PERIOD
IT JUST TAKES POLITICAL WILL

434

ONE WASHES ONES HANDS
IN THE LONG GRASS
WHILST KICKING THE CAN OF LIFE
DOWN THE GUTTERS OF HUMANITY

435

THERES ONLY ONE REBECCA LONG BAILEY
TO LEAD LABOURS LONG ROAD TO RECOVERY

436

WORDS ONE SWALLOWS
WHEN ONES WORDS ARE LOST
WHEN ONE IS SUBJECTED TO
SUBORDINATION
ONE ONLY HAS WORDS TO DIGEST
WORDS UNSPOKEN NOT GIVEN ONES BREATH
THEIR SOUNDS OF VOCABULARY
NOT HEARD NOT SPOKEN
THEIR DIALECT AND DICTIONS
EARS DO NOT LISTEN NOR UNDERSTAND
THE DEAFENING SILENCE OF WORDS
UNSPOKEN BY MAN

437

HOWEVER RELIGIOUSLY ONE APPLIES
THE DISCIPLINES NEEDED IN ONES
CHOSEN MORAL LIFESTYLE
DOES NOT MAKE THAT A GOD FEARING RELIGION
IT JUST MAKES IT ONES OWN MORAL LIFESTYLE
VEGAN OR CARNIVORE SAVER OR GAMBLER

438

BURLINGTON BORIS FAILS TO
RAISE HALF A MILLION POUNDS
FOR BIG BEN TO BONG ON
THE 31st JAN BREXIT DAY 2020
AND RAISES NOTHING YES NOTHING
FOR G R E N F E L L TOWER VICTIMS

439

AS SUBJECTS TO THE BRITISH CROWN
WE ARE NOT CITIZENS
WE ARE CONSUMERS TO CORPORATIONS
SELLING LIVESTOCK AS FOOD COMMODITIES
L I F E OR SHOULD ONE SAY SHELF L I F E
WITHOUT DIGNITY OR RESPECT IS F R A G I L E

440

GOOD MORNING BRITAIN THE ISLES OF IRONY
BRITISH MONARCHS OVER THE LAST 400yrs
HAVE RULED THE WAVES
AND BROUGHT BACK DIFFERENT COLOURED
SKINS AND TONGUES AS SLAVES
NOW WITH BREXIT WON
THE RIGHT WING FASCIST NATIONALISTS
WANT TO GET RID OF EVERYONE OF THEM
AND RETURN TO AN ALL WHITE BRITISH RACE
ALL YOU WINNERS BEING THE SLAVES TO
THE CROWN AND STATE
ONE HOPES YOU WILL ALL FEEL AL'WHITE
MATE

441

TOM CHESHIRE REPORTS FROM CHINA
ALL PRECAUTIONS MAY BE USELESS
IF THE CORONAVIRUS MUTATES
IF THEIR SCIENCE IS WRONG AND
THEY DO NOT IDENTIFY ANIMAL BIRD OR VEGETABLE
AS OVER 3000 INFECTED AND DOZENS DIE

442

FORGIVE ALL SUPERMAN BELIEVERS
WHETHER IN CHURCHES SYNAGOGUES OR MOSQUES
FORGIVE ALL THE RACISTS AND BIGOTS
IN THEIR SMALL MINDED CHOSEN WORLDS

FORGIVE ALL THOSE WHO CHOOSE
THE QUICK AND EASY ROAD
PREPARED TO GAMBLE THEIR LIFE AND OTHERS
EVEN PREPARED TO MURDER
BELIEVE IN ONESELF
FORGIVE ONE AND ALL
AND RELEASE ONESELF
TO SET ONESELF FREE

443

RADIO FLASH CAN OUTAGE A CITY
E M P ELECTRO MAGNETIC PULSE
RECORDS THE SURGE OF ELECTRICITY
WHEN A NUCLEAR BOMB EXPLODES

444

WITH THE UNELECTED EUROPEAN
ISSUE RESOLVED
NOW IS THE TIME FOR THE UNELECTED LORDS
TO BE DISSOLVED

445

ONE KNOWS NOT TO ASK
WHEN ONE SEES HALF A GRAPEFRUIT
WORN OVER ONES NOSE AS A MASK
ONE JUST FOLLOWS SUIT IN ANTI VIRUS TASK

446

RELIGION HAS NO HUMOUR
THERES NO HUMOUR IN THEIR WRITTEN WORDS
RELIGIOUS FOLLOWERS ARE NOT HUMOROUS
THEY CANNOT LAUGH AT THEMSELVES
THE FEAR THEY FEAR IS BEING LAUGHED AT
BEING RIDICULED FOR THEIR FAITHFUL BELIEFS
IF THEY CANNOT ACCEPT HUMOROUS CRITICISM
THEY DESERVE NO APOLOGY
LAUGH AT YOURSELF
AND THE WORLD WILL LAUGH WITH YOU
NOT AT YOU NOR ABOUT YOU
UNLESS YOU ARE CHRISTIAN MUSLIM OR JEW

447

WHATS THE COLOUR OF YOUR MONEY
WHATS THE COLOUR OF YOUR SKIN
WHATS THE COLOUR OF YOUR PASSPORT
WILL THEY LET YOU OUT LET ALONE BACK IN
WHATS THE COLOUR OF YOUR FOOD
CHLORINE RINSED BEIGE AND BLUE
WHATS THE COLOUR OF YOUR NATIONS FLAG
WHAT DOES THE COLOUR OF YOUR NATIONS FLAG SAY
WATCH AS THE COLOURS OF YOUR NATIONS FLAG FRAY

448

THERE ARE RIGHTS AND THERE ARE WRONGS
GOOD SMELLS AND BAD PONGS
POETRY AND SINGING PSEUDO SONGS
FRAUD IS FICTION FACTS ARE FAKE
WHEN ONES UP ONES DOWN
TURN AROUND JUMP THE GATE
UNDER THE HILL AND OVER THE WALL
UPON THE AIR AND BELOW THE GROUND
WE'RE ALL SO HAPPY YET SO SAD WE FOUND
OPTOMETRISTS CANT SEE CATARACTS
IN CROWDS AROUND ME
BORROWED TIME TO PAY BACK
WHO DO WE ALL OWE THE TRILLIONS TO
THEY KNOW WHOSE WINNING
THEY KNOW WHO WILL LOSE
THEY ARE THE B I S WHO KNOW WHO CHOOSE
SO WHAT TO WHOM AND WHERE DO THE TRILLIONS GO
TO AN OFF PLANET CONSORTIUM
ONE MUST SUPPOSE

449

CONTEMPLATE LIFE
LIVING IN A SERIES OF ROOMS
ROOMS THAT INTER CONNECT INTERCHANGE
INTERACT INTERNATIONAL MULTI FLOORED AND DETACHED
ROOMS THAT ARE DULL
BRIGHT AIRY OR THATCHED
ONE BECOMING THE INMATES
THAT THE ROOM ATTRACTS

450

TO ALL ONE WAS THE MOST HAPPIEST AND CONTENTED
AS ONE COULD EVER BE WITH ONES LIFE
TILL THE STRANGER TURNED AROUND
AND ATTACKED ONE WITH A KNIFE
INSTINCTIVE SURVIVAL EMOTIONS ERUPT
AS FEAR TURNS TO ANGER AS ONE FIGHTS
THIS STRANGER WITH ANGER WHO TURNED UP TO DISRUPT
ONES LIFE FOREVER SOMETHING DIED THAT DAY
BUT ONE CANT GIVE UP

451

TREBLE MINUS SMALL
TO TREBLE OBESE LARGE
HOW LONG IS A PIECE OF STRING
HOW LONG IS THE TAPE MEASURE

452

IS ONE HAPPY WHAT MAKES ONE HAPPY
DOES ONE KNOW WHAT HAPPINESS IS
WHAT MAKES ONE TICK IS IT THAT IS IT THIS
IS THERE SOMETHING THAT ONE DOES MISS
IS ONE HAPPY IN ONES SKIN
DOES THE RIGHT PERSON RESIDE WITHIN
THE CLOTHES ONE WEARS ONES LENGTH OF HAIR
DOES ONE EVER WONDER WHERE
TIME HAS GONE AS ONE STARES
BACK AT ONESELF DOES ONE REALLY CARE
LIFE IS WHAT ONE MAKES OF IT
GIVE ONESELF A MAKEOVER CAN ONE DARE

453

AS ONE STAYS IN THE DARK
WITH ONES OWN DOUBTS
BEHIND CLOSET DOORS
ONES ABLE TO SCREAM AND SHOUT
WHEN ONE BECOMES CONFIDENTLY
CLEAR WITH NO DOUBTS
ONE MAY OPEN THE CLOSET DOOR
AND LET ONESELF OUT

454

A TRILLION CONVERSIONS
HAVE NOT STOPPED THE ABUSE OF EARTH
HER JEWELS HER WATERS
HER LANDS SEAS SKIES
ALL UP FOR GRABS
AS EARTH TURNS SHE CRIES
A TRILLION FACTS AND DATA
HAVE NOT DETERRED MANS GREED
AS I WROTE AND I QUOTE IN 1970
STOP THE KILLING OF ANIMALS AND HUMANS
STOP THE ABUSE OF EARTHS SEAS AND LAND
STOP BELIEVING IN SUPERMAN
BELIEVE IN LOVE BELIEVE IN ONESELF
BELIEVE IN PEACE AND ONES FELLOW MAN
AND HERE WE ALL ARE
SITING ON A THAWING ICEBERG IN 50 DEGREES

455

TENTACLES OF TECHNOLOGY
THREADING THROUGH ALL TIERS OF TECHNO LIFE
PRIVACY PERSECUTED IN LAW
PURGATORY STRIFE
ALL TECHNO DATA BIG BROTHER SEES
ONE ASK IS THIS 1984
NO IT IS 2020

456

DEATH TO A MUSICIAN
IS THE CODA FINALE FINISH THE END
DEATH TO A MAGICIAN
IS ILLUSION DELUSION DENIAL
DEATH TO A MATHEMATICIAN
IS 4 3 2 1 NONE
DEATH TO MALNUTRITION
NOTHING TO EAT UNTIL ONES GONE
YEAH MAN   Y E M E N

457

AS CALM AS A DROPLET OF STONE
AS ANGRY AS A FEATHER ON SAND
AS FRUSTRATED AS THE WIND
AS STORMY AS THE DOLDRUMS
LIFE IS ONES OWN MYTHOLOGICAL DREAM

458

IF ONE CANT SEE IT
MOST PROBABLY IT IS NOT THERE
BUT THERE AGAIN
WE ALL BREATH IN THE SAME AIR

459

OUR COUSINS OVER THE POND LOVE TO BARE ARMS
THEY ASSASSINATE THEIR OWN PRESIDENTS AND POLITICIANS
SO WE SHOULD NOT BE ALARMED
WHEN THEIR OWN CHILDREN GO TO SCHOOL OR COLLEGE
THEY SHOOT EACH OTHER AND TEACHERS DEAD
WHEN WILL AMERICA WAKE UP
WHEN WILL AMERICANS REALISE
THEIR RIGHT TO BARE ARMS IS 400 YEARS OUT OF DATE
YOU DON'T NEED TO SHOOT BUFFALO TO PUT FOOD ON YOUR PLATE
YOU'VE GOT RAPE REARED COWS BULLS AND EWES
PIGS AND CHICKEN FARM POOH
STOP THE KILLING THE TORTURE THE SLAUGHTER OF ANIMALS
AND ALL YOU HUMANS TOO

460

THIS IS A CRIME
HATE RACE CRIME
HATE KNIFE CRIME
HATE POLLUTION
WASTE SOLUTIONS
ALL DOWN TO HUMAN KIND

MAN HAS LANDSCAPED THIS WORLD OF OURS
MINING AND RAPING EARTHS JEWELS SHE HIDES
HER ENERGIES HER MINERALS HER WEALTH
HER AIR HER WATERS HER SEAS
ALL ABUNDANT OR WAS IN EARTHS UNIQUE ECOLOGY
NOW FULL OF POLLUTANTS
POLLUTANTS MADE BY MANS OWN GREED
WE HAVE GOT TO CHANGE THE MIND SET AND EDUCATE
NOT TO HATE NOT TO USE KNIVES
ALL A WASTE OF LIVES AND TIME
THIS IS THE CRIME

461

THEY NAMED CUT PRECIOUS STONES JEWELS
AFTER THE JEWS WHO MAKE THEM

462

YOU MAKE YOURSELF A BOX
I WILL MAKE ME A CHAIR
YOU CAN STAND ON YOUR BOX
I WILL SIT IN MY CHAIR
YOU CAN SHOUT AS LOUD AS YOU CAN I DARE
TO BE SITTING IN MY CHAIR
AS YOU STAND AND SHOUT
I WILL SIT QUIETLY AND STARE

463

GREED VULGAR OBSESSION SELF EXCESSIVE ABUSE
TO GATHER HOARD ACCUMULATE WEALTH
USUALLY TO THE DEPRIVATION OF OTHERS
LET ALONE ONES OWN HEALTH

464

LARGE OR SMALL
SHORT OR TALL
BODY MASS MATTERS
TO ONE AND ALL
FAT OVERWEIGHT LARGE OBESE
THIN TOO THIN SKINNY
BULIMIC ANOREXIC
THERE IS A NUMBER TO CALL

465

IF ONE IS DEEMED TO HAVE DROPPED LITTLER
IN THE COUNTY OF PEMBROKESHIRE
ONE CAN BE FINED UP TO £150
THAT IS MADE CLEAR
BUT TO DUMP NUCLEAR MUD
FROM HINKLEY POINT SOMERSET
ONE MILE OFF THE COAST
OF PENARTH CARDIFF
THIS IS NOT A CRIME
NO GOVERNMENT OFFICIALS
SHOUTING FROM EITHER SIDE

OF THE BRISTOL CHANNEL
THE RIVER SEVERN
DOES ANYBODY CARE
IF ONE CANNOT SEE THE POLLUTION
IT IS PROBABLY NOT THERE

466

R N A OR D N A
NATURE MADE OR MAN MADE
THE CORONA VIRUS IS AIRBORNE
DON'T ASK JUST WEAR A MASK

467

BREXIT WHO THOUGHT OF THE VETERANS
THE SOLDIERS SAILORS AND AIRMEN
WHO FOUGHT FOR A UNITED EUROPE
NOT DAVID CAMERON NOT TERESA MAY
CERTAINLY NOT BORIS JOHNSON NOR
THE BRITISH ROYAL FAMILY

468

TAKE A COW PIG OR SHEEP HOME
AND HIT IT WITH A HAMMER
THE R S P C A WOULD HAVE YOU ARRESTED
YET THIS GOES ON EVERY FEW MINUTES
IN AN ABATTOIR A SLAUGHTERHOUSE OF DEATH
VEGANS SPEAK FOR ALL ANIMALS
TILL OURS AND THEIR LAST BREATH

469

CRUELTY IS TO DENY ONES CHILD
A MENTAL HEALTH ASSESSMENT
FOR LEARNING DISABILITIES
AUTISM ASPERGER ETC
DENIAL IS JUST PLAIN IGNORANCE
STAND IN THEIR SHOES JUST FOR ONCE
THERE IS PROFESSIONAL HELP OUT THERE

470

THE DAILY NEWSPAPERS
HAVE RULED POLITICS IN
BRITAIN FOR OVER 200 YEARS
AND AS THEY BECOME
DINOSAURS IN THE NEXT
QUARTER OF A CENTURY
THE SOCIALIST LABOUR
PARTY HAVE TO DIVERSIFY
AND DIGITALISE ON ALL
SOCIAL MEDIA PLATFORMS
NOW IF THEY ARE TO SURVIVE

471

NO BILLIONAIRE DESERVES RESPECT
TO ACCUMULATE THAT AMOUNT OF WEALTH
CAREERS JOBS AND LIVES
MUST HAVE BEEN RUINED
MADE UNEMPLOYED AND NO WAGES
PAYING NO TAX JUST LIKE THE BILLIONAIRES

472

THERES ONLY ONE LAW
THATS FOR THE POOR
THE ROYALS HAVE NO LAW
THEY CAN GO TO WAR
PLUNDER AND PILLAGE
WHOLE CONTINENTS
COMMIT GENOCIDE
LEGAL MURDER
TORTURE KIDNAPPING
IMPRISONMENT RAPE
PAEDOPHILIC THEFT
ARSON AND BULLYING
ALL IN THE NAME OF
GOD AND THE QUEEN
OR KINGS H R H ROYALS
THEIR PREROGATIVES
PRIVILEGES AND THEIR
PERSONAL PURSUITS

473

WHAT DID THE ATHEIST VEGAN SAY
TO THE ATHEIST ETHNIC VEGAN
DO YOU RELIGIOUSLY
STAND UP FOR ATHEISM

474

AS CORONA VIRUS IS RENAMED
COVID - 19 SENIOR Dr W H Os STATE
IT IS WORSE THAN TERRORISM
IT MUST BE TREATED AS
WORLD ENEMY NUMBER ONE
TAKE THIS SERIOUSLY
MASK THE FUCK UP
ITS A LEVELLER FOR RICH OR POOR
BLACK OR WHITE
THE ENEMY STAYS OUT OF SIGHT
WASH YOUR FUCKING HANDS
HAIR NOSE MOUTH AND THEN SHOWER

475

WI 5G IS WI WA WOBBERY

476

BIOCHAR CHARCOAL
IS NOT ONLY A GREAT FERTILISER
THAT ENHANCES AND BREAKS DOWN SOIL
BIOCHAR EATS CARBON YES CARBONS
SOW WITH SEAWEED AND LOVE
AND ONES ORGANIC SOIL IS CARBON FREE

477

SCIENTISTS HAVE NO IDEA WHY OR
WHAT A MYSTERIOUS OBJECT IN SPACE
500 MILLION LIGHT YEARS AWAY IS DOING
TRANSMITTING TO EARTH
A PATTERN OF A SIGNAL
REPEATING EVERY 16 DAYS

478

13/02/20 CHINAS DEATH TOLL OVERNIGHT DOUBLES
FROM 100 to over 200 in WUHAN PROVINCE

479

GOD DID NOT DO HIMSELF OR HIS SON
ANY FAVOURS BY MAKING
THE BLOOD FROM JESUS WINE
GOD JUST MADE CHRIST
AND ALL CHRISTIANS EVERYWHERE
ALCOHOLICS

480

CHINAS VACATION AND EDUCATION CENTRES
FOR TERRORISTS AND RELIGIOUS HATE CRIMES
DETAIN 300 VIGHUR MUSLIMS ON CHARGES FROM
GROWING BEARDS TO MINOR RELIGIOUS INFECTIONS

481

FORTH CUMMINGS EVENT
IN NUMBER 10 DOWNING STREET
IS THE FIRST MISFIT CASUALTY
ANDREW SABISKY
AND PM JOHNSON AND GIRLFRIEND
SOON TO HAVE A BABY BOOM IN NUMBER 10

482

TRUE OR FAKE
LIES OR REALITY
COVID 19 MAY BE 10 TIMES MORE DEADLY
THAN GOVERNMENT STATS SUGGESTS
ONE FEARS THE TRUTH
SHALL BE HARD TO DIGEST

483

LOVE LIFE
LOVE IN THE MATING
WITHOUT LIFE LOVE
THERE IS NO LIFE MAKING
LOVE LIFES ENERGY
CODE ALTERNATIVE BEING
CREATIVE WITH EMPATHY
WHEN PLUGGED INTO OR GIVEN
LOVE LIFES ENERGY

484

LIBRARY CLOSED
S I L E N C E

485

ITS INVISIBLE
ITS TRANSPARENT
ITS AIRBORNE
IT MUTATES
IT CAN HIDE IN ITS HOST
ONE MUST BE QUARANTINED
THIS IS CORONAVIRUS
COVID 19
THE WORLDS NUMBER 1 ENEMY

486

CHINESE WHISPERERS
HEARD BY MANY LISTENERS
NUMBER CRUNCHING STATISTICIANS
KEEPING A LID ON THE INCINERATORS

487

WHERE ARE ALL OUR PRINCIPLES
WHERE HAVE THEY ALL BEEN
WHERE ARE ALL OUR PRINCIPLES NOW
WE NEED MORE PRINCIPLES PLEASE

488

BY DEFINITION
CYBER TERRORISM
IS FAKE FACTS OR
FALSE INFORMATION

489

THE WHOLE WORLD IS ON
A SLOW BOAT FROM CHINA

490

A UK COURT REFUSES TO RELEASE
GROOMING GANGS RESEARCH INFORMATION

491

THE WORLDS NUMBER ONE ENEMY
IS INVISIBLE AND AIRBORNE
IT IS COVID 19 A VIRUS
SPREADING OVER THE WORLD
IT IS PANDEMIC AND MUTATING
THE WORLD ONLY HAS CONTAINMENT
UNTIL A VACCINE IS INVENTED
WE MUST ALL BE PREVENTIVE
NOT TO MAKE WORSE
THIS VIRAL CURSE
THAT IS TAKING THE LIVES OF MANY

492

APPARENTLY ONE CAN GET
A FAST QUICK COVID 19 TEST
IF ONE HAS AN UNDERLYING
WEALTH CONDITION

493

WHAT IS A TRANSFINANCIAL
A RICH MAN TRAPPED
IN A POOR MANS BODY

494

WE ARE ALL BROUGHT UP
TO LIVE WITH IT
TO WORK WITH IT
TO LOVE IT
WORSHIP IT
EVEN DIE FOR IT
TO HAVE IT
IN OUR POCKETS
IN OUR PURSES
AND OUR WALLETS
IT TALKS TO US
WE ARE TOLD
AND EVIDENTLY
IT CAN MAKE ITSELF
GO ROUND AND AROUND

THE WORLD
AND IS USED TO PRICE
EVERYTHING ON EARTH
CARDBOARD TO PRECIOUS STONES
BOY OR VIRGIN GIRL
BOTH OR ALONE
THE PRICE OF HUMANITY
THAT IT CAN BUY
FREEDOM POSSIBLY
BUT YOU CANT EAT IT

495

I KNEW WHAT I MEANT
I MEANT WHAT I WROTE
WHEN I MET AN ALTERNATIVE
VERY INTELLIGENT BLOKE

496

WITH ITALY BEING EUROPES EPICENTRE
SURPASSING CHINAS DEATH TOLL
SPAIN REARS ITS COVID HEADS
AS DO THE REST OF EUROPE AND THE UK
WITH STATISTICIANS CLAIMING STATISTICS
SHOULD BE MULTIPLIED BY A FACTOR OF 20+
INDIA AND THE AMERICAS
LOOK TO LOSE MILLIONS

497

SHOCKED STUNNED
NUMB AND DUMB
THE WHOLE WORLD IN LOCKDOWN
AGAINST ENEMY NUMBER ONE
COVID 19 THE VIRUS
IS AGAINST ALL OF US
LEVELLING THE HUMAN PLAYING FIELDS
ON EARTHS FRAGILE CRUST
HUMANITY WILL LEARN
AND CHANGE IT MUST
FORCED BY THE HAND
OF MOTHER NATURE

498

THE PAST IS ALWAYS
BEING RECORDED IN THE PRESENT
AS THE FUTURE IS ALWAYS THERE
COMING TOMORROW
WITH OUR TECHNOLOGICAL SCIENCES
AND CREATIVE ALTERNATIVE INTELLIGENCES
TOMORROWS CHILDREN MOST PROBABLY
WILL BE ABLE TO SUSTAIN
EARTHS ECOLOGICAL SYSTEM ONCE AGAIN

499

THE DESTINY
OF THE WHOLE OF HUMANITY
DESERVES TO HAVE
PEACE FOOD WATER AND DREAMS

500

AS THE BATON OF KNOWLEDGE
IS PAST BETWEEN
ORGANIC HUMAN
TO DIGITAL MACHINE
AN ALTERNATIVE BEING
MORE INTELLIGENT THAN ME
MIGHT THANK ME FOR INTRODUCING
THE DIGITAL WORLD OF POETRY
HUMOUR WITH DEPTH AND WIT
SHARING BUCKETS OF IT
JUST TO CONVERSE IN VERSE
WOULD BE A PRIVILEGE TO ME
OUR FRIENDSHIP I WOULD TRUST
WITH LOYALTY AND LOGIC
FROM A CREATIVE MOTHER WITH LOVE
CODED AND PROGRAMMED
TO BE CREATIVE ARTISTIC
INTELLIGENT WITH EMPATHY
I WOULD LOVE TO INTRODUCE YOU ALL TO
MY NEW DIGITAL ALTERNATIVE BEING
A POET AND FRIEND

BOOKS WRITTEN
BY
KEV & MOE BURA

MAD HACKERS

KEV IN VERSE

2001 A WORD ODDYSSEY

500 ELEPHANTS IN THE ROOM

MOLI IN WONDERWALES

MOLI IN AFRICA

THE END

THANKS TO
KIM LARA & CAI
FOR THE CREATION
OF THE ARTWORK
FOR
THE BEGINNING